D0138615

THE WORLD OF MYTHOLOGY

CELTIC MYTH

A TREASURY OF LEGENDS, ART, AND HISTORY

First published in North America in 2008 by M.E. Sharpe, Inc.

Sharpe Focus
An imprint of M.E. Sharpe, Inc.
80 Business Park Drive
Armonk, NY 10504
www.mesharpe.com

Copyright © 2008 Marshall Editions
A Marshall Edition
Conceived, edited, and designed by Marshall Editions
The Old Brewery, 6 Blundell Street, London N7 9BH, U.K.
www.quarto.com

Library of Congress Cataloging-in-Publication Data

Harpur, James.
  Celtic myth : a treasury of legends, art, and history / James Harpur.
    p. cm. -- (The world of mythology)
  Includes bibliographical references and index.
  ISBN 978-0-7656-8102-7 (hardcover : alk. paper)
  1. Mythology, Celtic. 2. Civilization, Celtic. I. Title.

BL900.H37 2008
299'.16113--dc22

                                    2007006015

Originated in Hong Kong by Modern Age
Printed and bound in China by Midas Printing Limited

10 9 8 7 6 5 4 3 2 1

Publisher: Richard Green
Commissioning editor: Claudia Martin
Art direction: Ivo Marloh
Picture manager: Veneta Bullen
Design and editorial: Tall Tree Ltd.
Production: Anna Pauletti

Previous page: The slopes of Ben Bulben in Ireland, where the hero Diarmuid met his death.
This page and opposite: Mount Brandon in County Kerry is one of Ireland's highest mountains. Some say the mountain takes its name from Bran, the mythical voyager to the Island of Women; others say that it recalls the sixth-century Christian saint Brendan the Navigator.
Opposite: This Celtic bronze head was made in the fifth century B.C.E.

THE WORLD OF MYTHOLOGY

CELTIC MYTH

A TREASURY OF LEGENDS, ART, AND HISTORY

JAMES HARPUR

Sharpe Focus

an imprint of M.E. Sharpe, Inc.

CONTENTS

The Struggle For Ireland

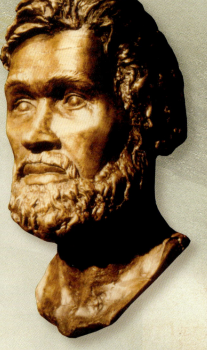

The Hound of Ulster and the Red Branch Knights

Heroes of the Fianna

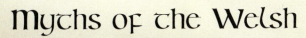

Myths of the Welsh

INTRODUCTION

The Celts—who originated in ancient Europe—produced one of the world's richest treasuries of myths. Full of magic, adventures, and love stories, Celtic tales open a window into a realm where heroes fought in ferocious battles; engaged in duels with warriors, giants, and animals; went on dangerous quests; and frequently fell in love.

The Celts' heartland was central Europe, but they were never a single, unified nation or empire. Rather, they consisted of a number of different peoples who shared a similar language, religion, and culture. The Celtic language varied from region to region, but it belonged to a family of languages known as Indo-European (which includes Greek, Latin, and Germanic tongues). The Celts' religion was polytheistic, which means that they worshipped a number of gods, many of them connected with nature and animals.

WHO WERE THE CELTS?

Because the Celts were not fully literate, our knowledge of them comes mainly from ancient Greek and Roman writers and archaeological discoveries. Scholars still debate exactly when a distinctive Celtic culture emerged in Europe, but it seems that by the ninth century B.C.E. an early form of Celtic art and culture known as Hallstatt (after an archaeological site in Austria) had begun to develop. Another style, known as La Tène (after a Swiss site) and characterized by swirling, geometrical patterns, was established during the fifth century B.C.E..

During the first millennium B.C.E., Celts migrated to various parts of the European continent, including France, Germany, Britain, and Ireland. Others reached Asia Minor (modern Turkey). It is not known exactly when these migrations took place, nor what these various Celts called themselves. The first reference to Celts in classical (Greek and Roman) literature is by the Greek historian Hecataeus in 517 B.C.E. He called them *keltoi* (from which we get "Celt"). The Romans had other names for them. They called Celts living in what is now France Galli, or Gauls, and those in Britain Britanni, or Britons.

Left: Dun Aengus is an ancient Irish stone fort that is perched 300 ft (100 m) above the Atlantic Ocean, on the island of Inishmore, lying off the west coast of Ireland. It was probably built at the start of the first century B.C.E. According to myth it was constructed by the legendary Fir Bolg people and named after their king, Aengus (dun means "fort").

During the last century B.C.E. and the first couple of centuries C.E., the Romans conquered most of the Celtic kingdoms. Roman civilization strongly influenced the Celts' culture. In Gaul, for example, as elsewhere, the Celtic language was more or less replaced by a form of Latin, the language of the Romans. In the fifth century C.E., however, Germanic tribes began to migrate westward and settle in parts of the crumbling Roman Empire, including areas where Celtic culture had been strong. The Celts then became confined to southwest England, Wales, Brittany (in northwest France), and, especially, Ireland, which was never invaded by the Romans. Celtic myths survived mainly in the Irish, and to a lesser extent the Welsh, traditions.

CELTIC MYTHS

Scholars still debate how and when Celtic myths—like those of other cultures—first arose and for what purpose. To some extent, they reflect religious rituals and record heroic deeds. They were also meant to entertain.

The myths began life being memorized by poets or storytellers, who would pass them down from generation to generation orally. We can imagine storytellers recounting their myths around a fire to a spellbound audience. The Irish Celts did have a written

Place of interest
Hill or mountain
Town
River
Borders

ATLANTIC
OCEAN

Orkneys

Skye

SCOTLAND

Iona

Lindisfarne

NORTH SEA

Tory. Island

SEA OF MOYLE

ULSTER

Ben Bulben   Navan Fort
Moytura   Slieve Fuad   Dundrum

Isle of
Glora

CONNAUGHT

Cooley
Peninsula

Lough
Derravaragh   Kells

Athlone

IRISH SEA

Lindow Moss

Boyne   Tara
Dublin
Valley of Thrushes

Aran
Islands

Shannon

LEINSTER

Hill of Allen

Snowdonia

Harlech

ENGLAND

IRELAND

MUNSTER

Lough Leane

CELTIC SEA

WALES

Dyfed

Servern

Gloucester

Pembroke

London

100 miles

100 km

language known as Ogham, but it was cumbersome and only used for short inscriptions. Then, after Christian monasteries were founded in Ireland and Britain from the sixth century C.E. onward, the stories were written down by monks on vellum, or calf-skin. These manuscripts were re-copied over the centuries, and often several different versions of the stories arose. The versions of the Irish and Welsh myths that have survived date mainly from the twelfth century and after. Because the original pre-Christian stories were written down by Christian monks, the myths tell of both a pagan world of heroes and gods and also, sometimes, an early medieval world, where Christianity has become established.

This book retells some of the best-known stories of the Irish and the Welsh Celts. It is divided into four chapters. The Irish Celts originally grouped their myths according to type, such as battles, adventures, voyages, and feasts. Modern scholars, however, have divided them into "cycles," or groups based around, for example, a theme or a place. The first three chapters of this book recount myths from what scholars have called the Mythological, Ulster, and Fenian cycles. The last chapter features tales from the Welsh collection of myths known as the *Mabinogion*, stories written down in medieval times but which draw upon much older myths and folklore.

One of the fascinations of modern Celtic studies is relating the old Celtic stories to facts about the historical Celts. Sometimes good parallels can be made. For example, classical writers refer to the Celts being fond of food, drink, and feasting, and the myths bear this out. On the other hand, it must be remembered that the myths are not history. They cannot be read as if they were the accounts of Ulysses S. Grant or Robert E. Lee remembering the American Civil War. So, for example, the stories of the heroes Cuchulainn (pronounced coo-hullin) and Finn Mac Cumhaill (fin mac-cool) may possibly have been based on historical Irish heroes, but there is no evidence for it. On the other hand, places mentioned in the Irish myths as royal centers, such as Tara in County Meath, often have archaeological remains that tally with the importance the stories give them.

In a broad sense, the stories do reflect aspects of ancient Celtic society. It was a world populated by many different tribes, each ruled by a king or chieftain. Warriors, priests, and poets were at the top of the social order, while peasant farmers were at the bottom. Priests, known as druids, were highly influential, and also acted as law-givers. Fighting played a central part in the Celts' lives. Cattle raids were common (as the story of the Cattle Raid of Cooley suggests), as were battles against other tribes. Champions would fight in single combat against each other, and loyalty to one's chieftain and people, as well as honor, were held in high regard.

Ireland is littered with *sidhe*, or "fairy mounds," where the legendary Tuatha De Danann were said to have lived. The *sidhe* are in fact manmade mounds that served as prehistoric burial places. This one is Dowth Passage Tomb in County Meath, originally dating from the third millennium B.C.E.

The Struggle For Ireland

The Mythological Cycle is one of the traditional groups of Irish myths categorized by modern scholars. The stories were written down in the Middle Ages—one of the cycle's major sources, the so-called *Book of Invasions*, dates to the eleventh century C.E.—but they reflect a much older, pre-Christian world. They tell of a mighty struggle between different peoples for dominance over Ireland. Down the centuries, scholars have debated whether any of these peoples corresponded with actual, historical invaders, but there is no certain evidence.

The original inhabitants of Ireland were said to be the Formorians, who successfully defended themselves against the invading Partholons and Nemeds. However, the next attackers, the Fir Bolg, presented a sterner challenge, and the Formorians were forced to make peace with them. The fourth invaders were the Tuatha De Danann (too-ha day danan), a magical, supernatural people, who married members of the Formorians. Despite the blood link connecting the two races, war broke out between them. This became a seven-year conflict that was finally won by the Tuatha De Danann at the second Battle of Moytura. Other stories in the cycle include the tragic tale of the Children of Lir and the story of Prince Midir's love for the beautiful Etain (eh-thaw-in).

THE BATTLE OF MOYTURA

One of the great battles of Irish myth, the Battle of Moytura pitted the supernatural Tuatha De Danann people, led by their hero Lugh (lew), against the formidable Formorians, whose champion, the giant Balor, possessed an "evil eye" that could kill people with a single glance.

The war between the Tuatha De Danann and the Formorians began after Nuada, the De Danann king, lost his hand while fighting in battle. The De Danann decided that it was not right to be ruled by a king with only one hand and chose a warrior named Bres to succeed him. Since Bres was the son of a De Danann mother and a Formorian father, they hoped he would maintain the peaceful coexistence between the De Danann and the Formorians.

But Bres turned out to be a bad king and treated the De Danann harshly. He gave them no royal hospitality or entertainments; they were made to pay heavy tribute to the Formorians; and their champions were reduced to performing humble tasks, such as digging trenches and carrying firewood.

Eventually the De Danann could stand it no longer and threatened to banish Bres. The king begged them to let him reign for a further seven years, to which they reluctantly agreed. But Bres had no intention of leaving his throne without a fight. One day he journeyed to the Formorians to raise a great army

Right: This bronze Celtic sword handle was made in the shape of a human figure. Although it was found in County Donegal in Ireland, it was probably forged in France during the first century B.C.E.

Right: Horses were crucial in Celtic warfare, both for carrying fighters and pulling chariots. This one, shown on a first-century C.E. British coin, is carrying an armed Celtic warrior.

with which to subdue the De Danann by force. Led by the grim champions Balor and Indech, this mighty Formorian host gathered to do battle with the De Danann.

FINDING A HERO

While Bres was away, Nuada was restored to the De Danann throne. And soon, a champion—the hero Lugh—presented himself at the gate of Nuada's court to lead the fight against the Formorians. Lugh was not allowed to enter until he had listed all the skills he had mastered. He told the gatekeeper he was a smith, a harper, a warrior, a poet, and had other talents, too. But the gatekeeper replied that the king already had men who fulfilled these roles. Lugh then asked whether there was any one man who, like himself, possessed all these different talents. The gatekeeper reported back to Nuada, who agreed to let Lugh enter. Before long Lugh had so impressed everyone with his strength and intelligence that he was made leader of the De Danann forces.

Preparations for the battle began on both sides. Among the De Danann there were men with specialist skills who promised to weaken the enemy—sorcerers who said they would fill them with fear, cupbearers who promised to make them thirsty, and druids who planned to dazzle them with showers of fire. The De Danann smith, Goibniu, said he would make brand-new weapons for every one that was broken, and would ensure that the spears he made would always hit their target.

THE CELTIC OTHERWORLD

When the Tuatha De Danann were eventually defeated by invaders of Ireland known as the Milesians, they went underground and lived beneath the grassy mounds known as "fairy mounds," or *sidhe* (shee). The Irish imagined this domain beneath the earth to be the Otherworld, a place inhabited by immortals. Sometimes they imagined the Otherworld existing on an island far away on the western seas, and at other times lying beneath the ocean. The Otherworld was usually described as a happy place, free from death and disease.

The Welsh called the Otherworld Annwn (an-noon). Like its Irish equivalents, it was a place where the boundaries were vague. Immortals could travel to the realm of mortals, and vice versa. For instance, in the Welsh tale about Prince Pwyll (poo-ihl), he and the lord of the Otherworld trade places in each other's domain for a year.

The Celts seem to have believed in a world existing beyond the frontier of death. In many Celtic graves the discovery of the remains of drink and food suggests that feasting was expected in the life to come.

THE EVIL EYE

On the day of the battle the two armies faced each other on the fields at Moytura (in present-day County Sligo). Lugh went up and down his battle lines, giving heart to each fighter with his inspirational words. The Formorians, too, were confident of victory, especially as they had Balor on their side. Day after day the two sides fought. Many fine warriors died, their bodies disfigured by swords and spears. Their blood made the ground underfoot slippery and reddened a river nearby. The Formorians were constantly amazed to see that their enemies' weapons, broken during the fighting, appeared soon afterwards in perfect shape.

In the thick of the battle, surrounded by the clash of metal and the splintering of wood, Balor managed to slay King Nuada. Now, using his terrible eye, the Formorian champion was ready to slay Lugh. Balor's eye was never opened except in battle, and it took four men to lift up the huge eyelid by using a handle attached to it. Once open, the eye gave off a poisonous force that would kill or render powerless all who fell under its horrific gaze.

Above: Tory Island, off the coast of Donegal in northwest Ireland, was where the terrifying Formorian champion Balor is said to have lived.

When Balor and Lugh at last faced each other, Balor ordered the eye to be opened. But just as the lid was being raised, Lugh cast a slingstone at it with all his strength. The stone hit the eye in the middle and knocked it right through Balor's head. Stone and eye fell on the Formorians, killing dozens of them. It was the turning point of the battle. The De Danann gained the upper hand and beat the Formorians back to the sea. That day the Formorian dead were as numerous as the stars in the night sky.

THE CHILDREN OF LIR

One time during the days of the Tuatha De Danann, a noble named Lir married the daughter of Bodb (bov), the king of the De Danann. The marriage proved a happy one. Lir and his wife, Eve, loved each other very much and had two children: a girl named Fionnuala (finoolah) and a son named Aed (ai). But then Lir's fortunes changed. Eve died while giving birth to twin sons, and Lir's world fell apart.

The widowed Lir was stricken with grief, as was Bodb, who had lost a beloved daughter. But after a while Bodb recovered his spirits and suggested to Lir that he marry another of his daughters, Aoife (eefah). Lir agreed, and for a while life was as good as it had been. His new wife was warm and loving, and at first she doted on her four stepchildren, Fionnuala and Aed, and the twins Fiachra and Con.

A CURSE

Yet, over time, Aoife became increasingly resentful of Lir's love for his children. The worm of jealousy grew inside her until she decided that something drastic had to be done. So one day she took the children off to her father's house, planning to get one of the servants to kill them in cold blood. When she failed to find anyone willing to carry out this terrible deed, she tried to do it herself—but her courage failed. Instead, she took the children to a nearby lake named Lough Derravaragh.

There, with the help of a druid's magic wand, Aoife turned the four children into swans. As she did so, she laid a curse upon them: they would spend 300 years on the lake, followed by a further 300 years by the Sea of Moyle in the north, then 300 years on the Isle of Glora in the west. However, she allowed them to keep their speech and to sing beautiful, unearthly songs. And she said they would only regain their human shape when they heard the sound of the bells of a new religion.

When Aoife's father found out the truth of what she had done, he used magic to banish her to the sky as a demon of the air. She was never seen again. But the curse she had placed on the children endured. Bodb and Lir, and other members of the De Danaan, would go to Lake Derravaragh and watch the four swans with a mixture of awe and sadness, listening to their human words and marveling at their sweet songs.

After 300 years, the swan children had to move on to their next destination: the Sea of Moyle in the north, where they lived beside the cliffs that overlooked the stormy, freezing waters. Here they experienced terrible loneliness and coldness, even though Fionnuala tried to protect her brothers from the weather by wrapping them in her wings.

Finally, their time by the sea came to an end and they flew off to their third and last destination, the Isle of Glora off the west coast of Ireland. Conditions on Glora were as harsh as by the Sea of Moyle, and the swan children suffered greatly. As their final period of imprisonment came to an end they decided to fly back to their father's palace to visit their old haunts. But as they neared the spot where his palace should have been, all they saw was grass, bushes, mounds, and trees—the buildings had long since crumbled away.

WHAT THE CELTS LOOKED LIKE

According to the Greek writer Diodorus Siculus (c. 90–30 B.C.E.), the Celts of Gaul were tall, well-built, and pale-skinned. They had naturally blond hair, which they made spiky and even blonder by washing it in chalky water. Some Celts were clean shaven, while others had beards or big, bushy moustaches, which, Diodorus claimed, they used as a sort of strainer when drinking! Celtic women were also tall, and they kept their hair long.

The Celts wore clothes made of wool or linen and colored by vegetable dyes. Tunics with long sleeves were common, as were trousers (although the Irish Celts probably did not wear them). Thick woolen cloaks kept out the winter cold. These had a check pattern and were fastened at the shoulder with a brooch.

Left: This stone head of a proud Celtic man shows him sporting a curled moustache. It was found in the village of Msecké Zehrovice in the Czech Republic.

A NEW RELIGION

The four swan children could do nothing but return to the Isle of Glora, sad that all trace of their former lives had disappeared. It was while they were living there that they first heard the sound of a Christian bell. For during their long exile, the Christian faith had come to Ireland. The bell now rang out in the chapel of a hermit, and to the ears of the children it sounded harsh and ugly. But the children got to know the hermit, who befriended them and told them about the new religion. He had a silver chain made that linked the four swans together. It seemed at last that the children had found a safe and friendly sanctuary after their hundreds of years of hardships.

But the children's new-found security did not last. A local king named Lairgnen married Deoca, a woman from the south of Ireland, and she came to hear of the marvelous swan children who talked and sang so beautifully. Deoca was determined to possess the swans and ordered her husband to capture them for her.

Lairgnen went to the hermit's chapel and stormed in. The swans took refuge on the altar, but the king marched up to grab them by their necks. As his fingers touched them, the swans suddenly turned back into their human forms—not as the beautiful children they had once been, but as withered, old people. Lairgnen was shocked and beat a hasty retreat from the chapel. Then Fionnuala, realizing that she and her brothers had very little time to live, asked the hermit to baptize them and bury them together. He agreed to do this, and the four children passed away peacefully, now joined together for eternity.

Below: This modern sculpture, in the Garden of Remembrance in Dublin, shows the children at the moment they were turned into swans by their stepmother.

Left: It was by Lough Derravaragh in County Westmeath that Aoife turned the four children of Lir into swans. They spent 300 years here before flying north to endure the next part of their curse.

Gods of the Celts

The Celts worshipped a large number of gods, many of whom were associated with nature. Unlike Greek and Roman gods, Celtic deities tended to be local: the Celts of Ireland, Britain, and Gaul (in present-day France) had their own special gods, connected with their own particular culture.

WORLD OF THE GODS

Some Celtic gods were probably more important and universal than others. The Roman general Julius Caesar noted five significant Celtic gods, which he identified with their Roman equivalents. One of them, for example, he named as the Roman god Mercury, describing him as the "inventor of all arts." This description fits the Irish deity Lugh (see pages 12–15), who was supposed to be a master of different arts, from fighting to playing the harp.

Artio
The Celtic goddess Artio was connected with bears, as is shown in this bronze statuette from Muri in Switzerland. Beside the goddess is a container full of fruit, suggesting that she was also associated with fertility.

Brigit
This first-century C.E. bronze head, found in France, is thought to represent the Celtic goddess Brigit. She was connected with prophecy, crafts, healing, and giving birth. When she was Christianized, Brigit kept many pagan associations. St. Brigit's feast falls on February 1, the same day as the pagan festival.

Cernunnos

Cernunnos, the antler-headed god, is shown here on a panel from the Gundestrup Cauldron (see pages 84–85). He holds a torc, or neck ring, in one hand, and a snake in the other. He is surrounded by other creatures, and scholars believe he was regarded as the "lord of animals."

Other Celtic gods were connected with animals. Artio was linked with bears, Epona was the goddess of horses, and Cernunnos was an antlered or horned god. In Irish myths, arguably the most important deity was the Daghda ("the good god"), a father-god and leader of the Tuatha De Danann, who wielded a large club. One of the Daghda's daughters was Brigit, who during Christian times evolved from being a pagan goddess to a Christian saint.

Left: This stone statue is double-headed and stands on Boa Island in Lough Erne, Northern Ireland. It is not clear what the statue represents or when it was made, but scholars believe it was a pagan Celtic idol. The figure has large bulging eyes and his arms are crossed. Local people still leave flowers and coins beside the statue.

MIDIR AND ETAIN

One day, a prince of the Tuatha De Danann named Midir was on his way to visit the god Aengus Og at his home at Brugh na Boinne (brew na bone-yer), beside the Boyne River, when he chanced upon a beautiful young princess named Etain. Midir fell in love with her immediately and took her to Aengus's dwelling place. There, forgetting about his wife, Midir lived with his new love for a whole year.

When Midir returned to his palace of Bri Leith (bree lay), he took Etain with him. Naturally, when his wife, Fuamnach (foo-am-nack), saw her husband sauntering home with a beautiful young woman, she burned with jealousy and decided to take her revenge. Fuamnach showed Etain into the guest bedchamber and, using magic, turned her into a pool of water on the floor. The heat from the fire in the room then changed the water into a beautiful scarlet fly, glittering like a jewel. The fly flew off to find Midir, who soon realized that it was Etain, and that Fuamnach was responsible for changing her form. Yet, although she no longer had a woman's shape, Etain was still a great comfort and friend to Midir.

Midir was angry with Fuamnach for what she had done, but not as angry as Fuamnach was for the way her husband still loved Etain. Fuamnach decided to get rid of Etain once and for all, and conjured up a great wind that blasted the fly out of the palace. Eventually it was blown to the home of the god Aengus Og. When Fuamnach found this out, she conjured up another wind to drive Etain out.

For seven years the fly was blown about the country until she arrived in the hall of an Ulster chieftain named Etar. There, exhausted, she fell into the wine cup of Etar's wife, who swallowed the fly along with her drink. Nine months later the woman gave birth to a daughter—whom she called Etain. And so in this way Etain was given a human form again.

Above: The prehistoric burial mound of Newgrange in County Meath is said to be the site of Brugh na Boinne, the palace of the god Aengus Og. The manmade mound was built in about 3200 B.C.E. and is circular, with a long passage that leads to a central burial chamber.

ETAIN REBORN

Just as she had been before, Etain grew up to become a striking beauty. She was so lovely that the High King of Ireland, Eochai (i-och-ee), made her his wife. They lived together at his palace at Tara. But their life of bliss began to unravel when the king's brother, Ailill (al-yil), also fell in love with Etain. This made Ailill so unhappy that he fell seriously ill. When Eochai had to go away, he instructed Etain to look after his stricken brother.

As she tended to him, Ailill confessed to Etain that he loved her. He pleaded with her to meet him outside Eochai's house and to share his love. Etain was torn. She did not want to betray her husband, but she did not want Ailill to die. After a great deal of doubt and confusion, she agreed to meet him. However, Ailill was overcome by sleep and missed their appointment. Twice more they arranged to meet, but each time Ailill overslept.

Yet, strangely, at each meeting Etain did see someone who looked just like Ailill. On challenging this mysterious person at the third meeting, Etain was amazed to hear him say that he was Midir, her old lover from long ago! Midir tried to persuade Etain to return with him to Bri Leith, but in vain. Yet he did not give up hope. Some time later, he returned and again begged her to leave with him, and at last Etain replied that she would go with him only if her husband gave her away. Midir agreed to this condition and left.

A CHALLENGE

Of course, Etain was sure Eochai would never give her away. But one day Midir returned to Eochai's palace and challenged him to a series of games of chess. Before the last game, the two men agreed that the winner could ask for anything he wanted. Midir won and asked for an embrace and kiss from Etain. The king was horrified, but agreed to let Midir have this in a month's time.

Midir duly returned and Eochai reluctantly allowed him to kiss his wife. As Midir did so, he clasped Etain, and both of them rose up into the air as two swans, leaving the castle by a skylight. They flew to Bri Leith, where they lived happily.

But Eochai was not finished. For nine years he tried to take Etain by force, and failed. Finally, to make peace, Midir told Eochai that if he could recognize his wife he could have her back.

Eochai was sure he could recognize her anywhere, but then Midir made sixty beautiful women, all looking like Etain, appear before the king. Eochai was taken aback, but felt he could pick out Etain by watching the women pour out wine. He made his choice and left, confident that he had chosen the right woman. Only when he was back at Tara did he discover that it was not Etain he had selected, but the daughter Etain had given him when they were together.

HOUSES AND VILLAGES

Celtic settlements varied from place to place. Some were simply a collection of houses, while others could be villages numbering between forty and fifty dwelling places. The most impressive settlements were royal centers, such as Heuneburg in Germany. Around the king's large residence would be clustered groups of houses where the ordinary folk lived.

Over time, streets with shops appeared. Julius Caesar called the Celtic settlements he found in Gaul *oppida*, or towns, and this is now the term scholars use. The buildings, whether large or small, were made of wood and sometimes stone. Typical construction consisted of timber frames, wattle-and-daub walls (upright stakes bound together with twigs and covered with clay), and sloping, thatched roofs. Stone walls were also built— without the use of mortar—if wood was scarce and the stone was easily come by. Inside, light was provided by the open door and by a central fire, which was vital for heat and for cooking. If the roof was high enough there was no need for a chimney hole: the smoke simply seeped into the thatch.

Left: This Celtic dwelling place, from about the first century B.C.E., has been reconstructed at Asparn in Austria. A central fire heated the room and the food.

THE VOYAGE OF BRAN

One day an Irish chieftain named Bran, son of Febal, was walking outside his fort when he heard strange, beautiful music wafting up behind him. The music was so melodic that it made Bran fall asleep. When he awoke, he found a strange silver branch with white blossoms lying beside him.

bran picked up the magical branch and returned to his fort. As he was showing the branch to the crowd that had gathered, a beautiful woman dressed in strange clothes appeared before them and began to sing a song about a distant island across the seas.

It was an island, she sang, surrounded by glittering seahorses. It had a beautiful plain on which games were played, with boats racing against chariots. Everywhere rainbow colors delighted the eye, and sweet music the ear. The land itself was well cultivated, and nothing but harmony reigned among the inhabitants—there was no grieving or treachery, no sorrow, sickness, or death.

The mysterious woman then urged Bran to set out immediately for this land, the Island of Women. She held out her hand and the branch that Bran had been holding leapt from his hand to hers. Then she suddenly vanished, as mysteriously as she had appeared.

THE ISLE OF JOY

The following day, Bran got ready to depart. Taking twenty-seven men, he launched his ship into the unknown seas to the west of Ireland. For two days the voyage was uneventful. Then, on the third day, they saw a chariot coming toward them over the waves. In it was Manannan, god of the sea, who began to sing a song. In his ballad he explained that what Bran saw as a clear, blue sea was for him a flowery plain. Whereas Bran could see only waves, he himself saw red flowers, glistening seahorses, and rivers flowing with honey. The sea god then encouraged Bran to row steadily to the Island of Women, which he would reach before sunset.

ST. BRENDAN THE NAVIGATOR

Another Irish figure who, like Bran, is supposed to have gone on a voyage to an island paradise was the Christian saint Brendan the Navigator (c. 486–578 C.E.). His legendary adventures were first written down in Latin during the tenth century in a book called the *Voyage of Saint Brendan*. This anonymous account was translated into French, Breton, Flemish, Welsh, and many other languages.

Brendan set out from southwest Ireland with seventeen fellow monks on a voyage that lasted seven years. Unlike Bran, they landed on many islands. On one they found food and drink laid out for them (but there were no people around), while on another they discovered sheep the "size of bulls."

Eventually the monks arrived at their destination: the Island Promised to the Saints. They explored the island for forty days and finally reached a river where a mysterious young man appeared. He blessed them and said they should now return home. They arrived back in Ireland and, unlike Bran and his men, were able to step ashore unharmed. There they told their brethren of the adventures they had experienced.

Above: This thirteenth-century illumination shows Brendan and his men after they had landed on the back of a whale. The sailors mistook the creature for an island, until they lit a fire and the whale began to move.

Bran rowed on and soon came to an island. It was not the Island of Women, but the Isle of Joy. There he saw large numbers of people staring and laughing at him and his men. As Bran circled the island, all he could hear was laughter. Mystified by this strange place, he sent one of his men ashore to investigate. In no time at all, the sailor had joined the crowd and, like them, had begun to laugh at his shipmates, refusing to rejoin them.

THE ISLAND OF WOMEN

Bran and his men rowed off and shortly reached the Island of Women. As Bran was wondering about landing there, a woman from the shore tossed him a ball of thread, which stuck to his hand. The woman then began to pull the thread and drew Bran's boat to the island. There, the Irishmen were given a royal welcome. Each man had his own bed in a large palace, and food, drink, and entertainment were plentiful. They were so happy that they forgot about their homeland and the passage of time.

But eventually one of Bran's crew, a man named Nechtan, got homesick. He pleaded with Bran to sail back to Ireland. The women begged them to stay, but in the end Nechtan managed to persuade Bran to return home. The Irishmen departed with a warning from the women that they had to rescue their shipmate from the Isle of Joy and that they must not set foot on Irish soil.

THE HOMECOMING

Bran duly picked up his crewman from the Isle of Joy—by this time he was ready to see his homeland again—and soon arrived off the west coast of Ireland.

On the shore a crowd of people shouted out to the ship, asking who they were. Bran bellowed back that he was "Bran, son of Febal." The crowd replied that the only Bran they knew was a character in one of their ancient stories: it was about a man who had set out on a voyage in search of the Island of Women and had never returned.

As it dawned on Bran and his men that they had been away from their homes for centuries, Nechtan leaped from the boat and waded toward the shore. But as soon as he touched dry land he turned into a pile of ashes, as if he had been buried in the earth for hundreds of years. The sailors were horrified to see their friend destroyed in this manner, and no one else left the ship. Then Bran told the people on the shore all about his voyage, so there would be a record of it. When he had finished, he said goodbye and sailed off over the seas. He was never seen again.

Below: This gold ship, about 4 in (10 cm) long, was found in a bog at Broighter in Derry, Northern Ireland. It represents an ocean-going vessel and may have been intended as a gift to a sea god.

Many of the myths of the Ulster Cycle took place in the countryside of Northern Ireland, including the Mountains of Mourne, in King Conchobar's kingdom.

The Hound of Ulster and the Red Branch Knights

The second traditional division of Irish myths is known as the Ulster Cycle. The stories take place within and near the borders of the province of Ulster in the north of Ireland. The hero of many of these tales is Cuchulainn (coo-hullin). He was originally called Setanta, but after killing the ferocious hound of a man named Culann, he changed his name (Cuchulainn means "hound of Culann").

Cuchulainn's exploits are often connected with King Conchobar (con-cor-vor) of Ulster and his Red Branch knights—of whom Cuchulainn was to become the champion. In particular, the Ulstermen were involved in a war against Medb (maeve), queen of the province of Connacht, and her husband Ailill (al-yil). The conflict started as a result of Medb's attempt to steal a bull from the Ulstermen, an episode known as the Cattle Raid of Cooley. It then turned into a bitter, bloody war, which cost the lives of many heroes.

CUCHULAINN
COMES TO MANHOOD

The greatest of the Ulster heroes, Cuchulainn, was born to Dechtire, the sister of Ulster's King Conchobar, and the De Danann hero, Lugh of the Long Arm. For the first seven years of his life the young boy was called Setanta. He grew into a strong, brave lad and it was not long before he wanted to join the troop of boy warriors established at the king's fort.

Setanta's mother told him he was too young to join the king's troop. But, against her wishes, he left home and set out for Conchobar's fort at Emain Macha (evin macha). He took with him a toy shield, his hurley (a stick used in the game of hurling), and a ball. He shortened his journey time by hitting the ball way up into the air then running along to catch it before it touched the ground.

JOINING THE GAME

Setanta eventually arrived at Emain Macha, where he saw the boy warriors playing a game of hurling. Without waiting to be asked, Setanta joined their game and soon scored a goal. The boys were furious at this bold interruption and threw their hurley sticks at him. But Setanta dodged them all. They threw balls at him, but he deflected them. They threw their spears, and he parried them with his toy shield.

Setanta then got so angry at this bullying treatment that he went into a battle frenzy. His hair stood up like nails. His face became grotesquely distorted, with one eye shrinking to the size of the eye of a needle, the other widening to the size of a bowl. And his teeth were bared through his gaping mouth. Above his head shone a deep, glowing warrior light that would appear whenever he was in such a frenzy. He launched an attack on the boys and routed them. Eventually the boys agreed to his demand that he should be their protector—even though he was only seven years of age.

Above: Navan Fort in Armagh, Northern Ireland, is said to be the site of Emain Macha, the home of King Conchobar. It was here that the king and his Red Branch warriors held sway over Ulster.

THE HOUND OF CULANN

Setanta settled in at Conchobar's household and soon gained a reputation as a great warrior. Then, one day, a blacksmith named Culann came to the king and invited him to his fort for a feast.

The king accepted the invitation and asked Setanta to join him. Setanta agreed to come after he had finished the game of hurling he was playing. So the king set out with his men and eventually reached the blacksmith's home. When all the guests were sitting at the table ready to eat, Culann asked Conchobar whether all his men were present. Forgetting that Setanta had not yet arrived, the king replied that all of them were there. Culann then let loose his ferocious wolfhound to stand guard outside the fort to protect the diners.

Meanwhile, Setanta had finished his game of hurling and was making his way to the feast. As he neared Culann's home, he saw a huge snarling hound charging at him. Wielding his hurley stick, Setanta smashed a ball into the hound's throat. He then picked the creature up by its legs and broke its head on the ground.

Above: Setanta stands triumphantly over the hound of Culann in this early twentieth-century illustration by the artist Stephen Reid. After killing the hound, Setanta was renamed Cuchulainn and soon became Ireland's greatest warrior.

When the king heard the roar of the hound, he suddenly remembered Setanta and feared that the beast had savaged the boy. All the feasters rushed out to see what had happened. There, outside the fort, they found Setanta standing triumphantly over the dead hound.

With a great cheer they took Setanta inside to celebrate. But Culann was not so happy. He was pleased that Setanta had survived the attack, but sorry that he had lost such a good guard dog. He now feared that his home would no longer be safe from thieves and raiders. But Setanta saved the situation by telling Culann that he would train another hound to protect his fort and that in the meantime he himself would guard him and his home. There and then Setanta was called Cuchulainn, the "Hound of Culann," and it was by this name that he became known as Ireland's greatest warrior.

One day, some time later, Cuchulainn was passing by a druid named Cathbad when he heard him say that the youth who took up arms on this day would become the most famous warrior in Ireland. However, his life would be short. Tempted by the idea of fame, Cuchulainn went to Conchobar and demanded to be given arms. So the king gave him two spears, but Cuchulainn shook and whirled them about to test them and ended up breaking them. The king gave him more weapons, but Cuchulainn broke these too. Finally, Conchobar gave him his own spears and sword, and this time Cuchulainn could not break them. In this way the young hero took up arms—and set in motion Cathbad's prediction. He would indeed achieve great fame, but his life would be all too brief.

THE ANCIENT GAME OF HURLING

Hurling is an ancient Celtic sport and still one of the most popular games in Ireland. Its long history is testified by the fact that it is mentioned in mythic tales featuring Cuchulainn. Modern hurling matches consist of two teams of fifteen players, or hurlers. Each player has a hurley—a wooden stick with a handle and a flat, broad blade. The idea is to hit a leather ball (about the size of a tennis ball) into the opponents' goal (for three points) or above the goal and between the extended goal posts (for one point). Hurlers can hit the ball over long distances, and it takes great skill for players to catch it with their hand or hurleys. With players from opposing teams challenging hard and smashing the ball around the pitch, hurling is not for the faint-hearted!

CUCHULAINN'S SON

Cuchulainn grew up in Ulster at the court of King Conchobar and his Red Branch knights, the warriors who fought for the king. In time Cuchulainn fell in love with a beautiful woman named Emer. But Emer's father, Forgall, did not like the idea of such a wild warrior as his son-in-law. So he persuaded Conchobar to send Cuchulainn far away across the seas to Scotland to learn the arts of war from a sorceress named Scathach (scaw-thach).

Conchobar thought this was a good idea and sent Cuchulainn to the Isle of Skye, off the Scottish coast, where Scathach had her fortress. After a difficult journey, the young hero finally reached her lair, and Scathach agreed to teach him the secrets of fighting. In particular she showed him how to throw a special spear called the Gae Bolga. This was thrown using the foot, and always hit its target.

Cuchulainn did not have to wait long before he could put his new-found martial skills to use. Scathach was at war with a ferocious woman warrior named Aoife (eefah) and her tribe, and the Ulster hero volunteered to join the fight against her. During a battle between the two armies, Aoife challenged Scathach to send her a champion to fight her in a duel. Scathach sent out Cuchulainn and, after fierce fighting, he overcame Aoife.

Cuchulainn not only spared Aoife's life but he also fell in love with her. Soon she became pregnant with his son. Cuchulainn, however, had to return to Ireland. He told Aoife that their son should be called Connla. He gave her a gold ring to put on Connla's thumb when he was old enough to fit it. At such a time, Cuchulainn instructed, Connla was to set out for Ireland to find him. The boy was to tell his name to no one, step aside for no one, and never refuse to fight a challenger.

Opposite: The craggy landscape of the Isle of Skye formed the backdrop for Cuchulainn's stay with the sorceress Scathach. Here she taught the fighting arts to the Ulster hero.

CONNLA ARRIVES IN IRELAND

Cuchulainn returned to Ireland and soon married Emer, against the wishes of her father. One day, seven years later, Cuchulainn, King Conchobar, and the other knights of the Red Branch were gathered on a beach, gazing at the sea, when they saw a shining bronze boat with golden oars approaching. Inside it a boy was firing his sling at birds and bringing them down alive. He would then release each bird into the sky and sing a note of such intensity that the bird would again fall down into the boat.

THE PICTS

When Cuchulainn was sent to Scotland to learn the arts of warfare he was going to a country well known to the Irish. By the sixth century C.E., there was a large settlement of Irish in the west of Scotland. They were vying for power and land with Romanized Celts to the south, and in particular with the Picts to the north.

The Picts are one of the most mysterious of ancient peoples. It is not clear what they called themselves. *Picti* is a Latin word meaning "painted ones," and probably refers to the Picts' custom of painting their bodies. They built forts on hills and lived in houses made of wood and stone. They also produced beautiful artifacts, including delicate silver brooches, and mysterious carved pictorial symbols, such as fish and deer, on large stones.

Conchobar was deeply worried. If a small boy could perform such a feat, the men of the boy's country would surely be invincible warriors. So he sent one of his men, Condere (condirrah), to use his diplomacy to stop the boy from landing on the shore. Condere set off and, at the shore's edge, asked the boy his name. The boy, of course, was Connla, and he replied that he would step aside for no one, refuse the challenge of no one, and would not reveal his name unless he was defeated in a duel.

Condere did not feel confident enough to challenge the boy and returned to Conchobar to report what had happened. Then another Red Branch knight, Conall, marched down the beach to confront the boy. But Connla answered his challenge by firing a slingshot—just its noise and the force of its wind knocked Conall over. Connla then tied Conall up before he could recover.

A TERRIBLE DUEL

Cuchulainn had been watching all this and now decided he had to end this mysterious boy's impudence. Yet Emer, who was by his side, pleaded with him not to go. Although she did not say so, she somehow guessed that the boy was Connla and she did not want to see her husband kill his only son.

Cuchulainn was deaf to her pleas. He strode out with grim determination and ordered the boy to reveal his name. Connla refused, and so father and son entered into mortal combat. First they fought with swords, and Connla, with supreme skill, cut off his father's hair with one swipe of his blade. Next, they wrestled, and again Connla got the better of his father. Finally they fought in the water. As Connla gained the upper hand, Cuchulainn went into his battle frenzy and launched his magical spear, the Gae Bolga, with his foot. The deadly missile hit its target and Connla fell, his blood mixing with the waves.

As Cuchulainn picked up the body of the dying boy, he suddenly saw on his thumb the gold ring he had given to Aoife. Grief-stricken, he brought Connla to the watching champions, who at first found it hard to believe that the young lad was Cuchulainn's son. But Connla, with his life ebbing fast, told them it was true and asked to embrace the famous Ulster heroes before he died. One by one they clasped him, with Cuchulainn the last to do so. Connla died in his arms.

Opposite: This eighth-century Pictish stone, on the Orkney Islands off Scotland, is carved with mysterious symbols. They include three Pictish soldiers, bearing square shields and spears. The stone may have marked a burial or perhaps a boundary.

BRICRIU'S FEAST

There was in Ulster a mischievous character called Bricriu (bree-croo) the Poison-Tongue, who liked nothing better than to make trouble between people. One day he decided to hold a great feast at his fort of Dun Rudraige (dun rory), to which he invited King Conchobar and his Red Branch knights. Bricriu's real aim was to get the men fighting among themselves.

Reluctant at first, because they suspected Bricriu's motives, the Ulstermen eventually accepted the invitation. As the knights traveled to his hall with their women and attendants, Bricriu began to work his trickery. First he went up to one of the Ulster champions, Loeghaire (leary), and flattered him, telling him that he alone was worthy to receive the champion's portion—the largest and best serving of food—at the feast. Bricriu persuaded Loeghaire to claim the portion when the time was right during the banquet. Bricriu then secretly went to two other heroes, Conall and Cuchulainn, and convinced them to do the same thing.

Later at the feast, when it was time to award the champion's portion, the charioteers of the three heroes all claimed it for their masters. As Bricriu had hoped, a vicious fight broke out between the three Ulstermen, who stopped only at the command of Conchobar.

THE BATTLE OF THE WIVES

Bricriu then turned his attention to the women. He persuaded the wives of the three heroes that the one who returned first to the hall after their evening walk would be counted first among the women. So, after the wives had strolled to a nearby ridge, they and their attendants began to walk back slowly to the hall. But as they got nearer to it they began to speed up—until in the end, they hitched up their skirts and raced to be the first back home! Although Cuchulainn's wife Emer arrived first, the doors were closed, and the heroes inside vied with each other to let their wives in. Eventually Cuchulainn managed to lift up the hall itself, allowing Emer to enter.

FEASTING AND FOOD

Below: This bronze flesh hook, found at Dunaverney in Northern Ireland, was probably used to take meat out of a boiling cauldron.

As the story of Bricriu's feast indicates, the Celts loved a good feast, with lots of eating and drinking. They were extremely hospitable, and complete strangers might be invited to share the food on offer. According to Roman and Greek writers, the Celts did give the best portion of meat to the man regarded as the finest warrior, and fights did break out over who should be given that honor.

The Celts ate a wide range of meat, including pork, beef, venison, and bear. Those living near the coast would also consume fish. For their vegetables, peas and beans were grown, and they also had grains such as wheat, oats, and barley, which could be turned into a type of porridge. Honey was gathered from bees and used to sweeten beer.

Right: Found in Lorraine in France, this Celtic flagon was used to pour beer, wine, or mead at banquets. Its handle is shaped like a dog or wolf, and there is a decorative duck on its spout.

Above: The ruined medieval castle of Dundrum in County Down, Northern Ireland, stands on the site of an older fort, where it is traditionally believed that Bricriu held his feast.

But the question of who should receive the champion's portion still had to be settled. It was decided to send the three heroes off to the court of Queen Medb and Ailill in Connacht and get them to judge who should receive it. After the men had arrived at her court, Medb took Loeghaire aside in private and gave him a bronze cup, telling him this was a secret token of his being the most worthy champion. But she then gave Conall a white bronze cup, and Cuchulainn something even more precious—a jewel-encrusted gold cup. Like Bricriu, Medb had tricked them, for each man believed that he had been appointed the winner.

The men returned to Emain Macha, and a banquet was held in their honor. When it was time to allot the champion's portion, each man sprang up to claim it—and, of course, a furious fight again broke out between them.

THE OGRE'S THREE CHALLENGES

It seemed they would never solve the problem, until one day a mysterious, grim-looking giant turned up at Conchobar's court. He carried with him a cudgel the size of a tree and a huge axe. As the court all wondered what this ogre wanted, the giant issued them a challenge.

In his great booming voice he said: "I'm looking for a man who will agree to cut off my head tonight, then allow me to cut off his head tomorrow night."

At first no one stirred. But then, when goaded by the giant, Loeghaire stepped forward and agreed to his terms. The giant then placed his head on the block and Loeghaire chopped it off with an axe. To everyone's astonishment, the giant got up, picked up his bloody head and walked out.

The next night the giant returned to chop off Loeghaire's head. But the Ulsterman was too scared to show up. So the ogre issued another challenge, and this time Conall responded. But the same thing happened. Conall cut off the giant's head and then failed to be present when the giant came back the next night. Scornful of the Ulstermen's courage, the giant then challenged Cuchulainn. The hero duly accepted and sliced off the giant's head.

When the giant returned the next night, Cuchulainn, although frightened, was ready to place his head on the block. As everyone held their breath, the giant took up his axe to a great height and brought it down toward the hero's outstretched neck. A gasp went up—but the giant had turned the axe blunt-side down and he stopped it before it had done more than gently touch Cuchulainn's skin. The giant congratulated Cuchulainn on his bravery and told him that he alone was worthy of the champion's portion.

DEIRDRE OF THE SORROWS

When Deirdre was born to the wife of Felimid, one of King Conchobar's bards, a druid predicted that she would grow into a woman of stunning beauty. But he added that she would also be the cause of fighting and great sorrow. Some of the king's men thought it best to kill the baby straightaway. But Conchobar decided to bring her up in a secluded place and to marry her himself when she was the right age.

Deirdre grew up into a beauty, unseen by the world except by her foster parents and a teacher named Levercham. One morning, as she was looking out of the window, she saw her foster-father skinning a calf on the snow. As the blood spilled out, a raven swooped down to drink it.

Deirdre turned to Levercham and said, "I would fall in love with a man whose hair was raven-black, whose cheeks were as red as blood, and whose skin was as pale as snow."

Levercham replied that there was a man named Naoise (neesha) who answered that description. He lived at the king's court at Emain Macha.

One day, Deirdre was in Emain Macha when she heard a man singing in a beautiful voice. It turned out to be Naoise. She went over to him and, as they looked at one other, each was seized by the other's beauty. They fell in love at first sight. But Naoise knew that Deirdre was betrothed to the king. When Deirdre urged him to run away with her, at first he refused, fearing the king's wrath. Deirdre appealed to his sense of honor, and in the end he agreed. Deirdre, Naoise, and his two brothers fled from Emain Macha, knowing that Conchobar would try to hunt them down.

The four fugitives roved around Ireland, staying in different places, then crossed the seas to Scotland. For a while they lived with the king of Scotland, but then they moved to a remote island because the Scottish king desired Deirdre for himself.

A SAFE CONDUCT

When news of their fate reached the Red Branch knights, they felt sad that such noble Irish warriors should be rotting away on a tiny island. So the knights asked Conchobar to pardon them and allow them to return to Ireland. The king agreed, and sent a message to Naoise and Deirdre, inviting them to return. Naoise and his brothers were overjoyed at the idea of going home. To guarantee their safety, they asked the king to send three champions, Fergus, Cormac, and Dubthach (duv-tah), to escort them. The king agreed to this, but in reality he was plotting the brothers' destruction. The three knights brought the exiles back to Irish soil. Meanwhile, Conchobar made an arrangement with one of his nobles whose fort lay on the route back to Emain Macha.

Left: Celtic women would have used ornate mirrors such as this one, which was found at Desborough in England. About 2,000 years old, it is made of bronze and richly engraved on its back.

CELTIC WOMEN

Celtic society was very much a man's world. Among the nobility, for example, chieftains would marry off their daughters to the leaders of other tribes to cement alliances with them. But occasionally women did achieve real political power. The Irish myths mention Queen Medb of Connacht as a strong ruler, and history records the reign of Boudicca (or Boadicea), queen of the Iceni tribe in Britain.

Mistreated by the Romans, who had conquered much of Britain, Boudicca rose in revolt in about 60 C.E. and destroyed several Roman garrison towns before finally succumbing to the might of the empire.

Celtic women probably wore simple fabric dresses, skirts, and cloaks. They made use of pins to style their hair in different ways. They wore bronze bracelets, gold neck-rings or torcs, and necklaces made of glass or amber beads.

In Roman times, earrings and finger-rings became more popular. Not much is known about Celtic cosmetics, but mirrors were certainly used. Made of bronze and iron, mirrors were often objects of great artistry. Their backs were adorned with intricate designs and enameling.

Right: The great British warrior Boudicca charges in her chariot in this sculpture near Westminster Bridge in London. Boudicca led a fierce rebellion against the Romans but was eventually defeated.

The noble agreed to hold a feast in Fergus's honor. The king knew that Fergus would feel duty bound to attend the feast. Naoise and Deirdre were greatly distressed when Fergus told them that he and his two companions had to leave them and attend the banquet. But he reassured them that he would send his son Fiacha (feeockah) to escort them in his stead.

When Deirdre, Naoise, and his two brothers arrived outside Emain Macha with Fiacha, they fell straight into the king's trap. Waiting for them was Eoghan (owen) of Fernmag, the son of a rival king with whom Conchobar was seeking peace, and a band of hired warriors.

Naoise went to greet Eoghan. But Eoghan caught him off guard and pierced his body with a spear. Naoise collapsed. Fiacha tried to cover Naoise with his own body, but Eoghan plunged his weapon through both men and killed them. Then the hired warriors proceeded to slaughter Naoise's brothers and attendants. Deirdre was seized and handed over to Conchobar.

FERGUS'S REVENGE

When Fergus heard the news of the massacre, he was outraged that Conchobar had broken his promise of a safe conduct and that his own son had been killed. After swiftly gathering together an army, Fergus attacked Emain Macha, killed hundreds of warriors, and set fire to the fort. He then left Ulster and took refuge with Queen Medb and Ailill in Connacht.

Deirdre was now the king's prisoner. For a year she refused his advances and lived in misery. The king realized that Deirdre hated him and Eoghan, murderer of Naoise. He decided to punish her by making her live with Eoghan for a year. But steadfast Deirdre managed to escape this fate.

One day, Conchobar and Eoghan were taking Deirdre to a nearby fair in the king's chariot. She saw a large rock by the side of the road, and as the vehicle passed it she leaned over and struck her head against it, dying instantly.

The Hound of Ulster and the Red Branch Knights   **47**

THE CATTLE
RAID OF COOLEY

One day Queen Medb of Connacht and her husband Ailill were talking about how much wealth they had. Ailill boasted that, although they had an equal amount, he also possessed a huge, healthy bull with white horns. Medb was jealous. She decided that she must get hold of a bull that would outdo her husband's.

When Medb heard that there was an Ulsterman from the district of Cooley who owned a magnificent brown bull, she decided she must have that beast. At first she tried to bargain for the bull. When that failed, she made plans to mount a great raid on Ulster to steal it. She was determined to take possession of the bull, and was prepared to do it by any means necessary.

Medb amassed a vast army from among her own people and from other parts of Ireland. The force included some Ulstermen who had fled from their province. When all the preparations had been made, Medb and her army advanced into Ulster. They did not expect much opposition because they knew that Conchobar and his men had been laid low by a curse. This curse lasted several months, during which time the Ulstermen felt sick and weak, and were unable to fight. Only one person had remained untouched by the curse, and that was Cuchulainn, Ulster's greatest champion.

As she had hoped, Medb was able to capture the brown bull of Cooley without much difficulty. But she still had to get the animal back to Connacht. And Cuchulainn had other ideas. With the honor of Ulster at stake, he fought single-handed with terrifying strength against the invaders.

Time after time, Medb's finest champions were sent to kill the "Hound of Ulster," but each time Cuchulainn got the better of his man. He knew that, if he could hold out for long enough, the soldiers of Ulster would recover from their illness and vanquish the enemy.

BATTLING WITH A FRIEND

As the days went by, Medb became increasingly frustrated by her lack of progress. Finally, she persuaded her greatest warrior, Ferdia, to fight Cuchulainn. Ferdia had trained with the Ulster hero under the sorceress Scathach on the Isle of Skye and knew all the same martial skills. The only thing that Ferdia lacked was the Gae Bolga, Cuchulainn's deadly spear.

The two men, who had been the greatest of friends, fought each other at a river ford in a struggle that lasted for a number of days. They would fight all day long, then when night came they would hug each other, only to start again the next morning.

They were so evenly matched that it seemed neither would win. Finally, just as Ferdia began to gain the upper hand, Cuchulainn launched the Gae Bolga with his foot and killed his friend. He then lay down, exhausted, wounded, and stricken with grief.

Below: Bulls were revered by the Celts, as the story of the Cattle Raid of Cooley suggests. This sculpture of a bull's head was found in a bog near Rynkeby in Denmark. It dates from the fourth century B.C.E.

THE ULSTERMEN FIGHT BACK

Shortly after Ferdia's death, the men of Ulster began to recover their health. With Medb's huge army still threatening Ulster, King Conchobar gathered a mighty force to fight them. The Ulstermen advanced to meet the enemy, and a great battle took place. Hundreds of fine warriors on both sides were slaughtered. Screams of pain and fury filled the air. For a while, Cuchulainn was too weak to join in. Eventually, when he saw Fergus, an exiled Ulsterman fighting for Medb, causing havoc, he stormed into battle, killing swathes of the enemy.

In accordance with a pact he and Cuchulainn had once made, Fergus retreated from the field. And as he left, forces from other parts of Ireland deserted Medb's army. She herself bravely entered the fray, and was nearly killed by Cuchulainn. He spared her life only because it was dishonorable to kill a woman. But Medb and her men were beaten. Next day, the sorry remnants of her army dragged themselves home, but they did manage to take the brown bull with them.

Back in Connacht, Medb was not even allowed to enjoy her prize bull—which she had taken at the cost of so many thousands of lives. For now it was this beast's turn to fight a battle. It attacked Ailill's white-horned bull. The two animals kept on battering each other, and it was the brown bull who won. Suffering from terrible gore wounds, the brown bull wandered off around Ireland before it finally dropped dead.

THE CELTS IN BATTLE

Celtic soldiers were armed with a number of weapons. The main ones were spears and 3-ft-long (1 m) iron swords. But they also used slings and bows and arrows. A few Celtic warriors wore armor, which usually consisted of chain mail and a bronze or iron helmet. Most men wore ordinary clothes. And there were even some soldiers who went into battle naked—scholars are not sure why, but they believe it was for some religious reason. To protect their bodies, Celts carried large wooden shields covered in leather.

Chariots played an important role in Celtic armies. Drawn by two strong horses, chariots ran on two wheels with iron tires. They were large enough to hold a driver and a soldier, who cast his spears then got out to do battle on foot.

Before a battle started, the Celts would blow trumpets, shout, and bang their shields to frighten the enemy. They would then launch themselves at their foes, hoping to scatter them. With thousands of screaming warriors running at full pelt, such charges must have been a terrifying sight. Only Roman armies, with their superb training, weapons, and discipline, proved to be the Celts' betters.

Right: This bronze shield, with its swirling designs and studs of red glass paste, shows the superb workmanship of the Celts. Its ornamentation suggests that the shield was kept just for ceremonies.

Death and Sacrifice

Over the years, well-preserved bodies from Celtic times have been found in peat bogs. Some of them have shown signs of human sacrifice. For example, in 1984 a male body was found in a bog at Lindow Moss near Manchester in England. It was discovered that Lindow Man, as he was called, had died from horrific wounds.

RITUAL SLAUGHTER

Lindow Man was hit on the head with an axe three times, strangled with a cord, and then had his throat slit. The elaborate nature of the man's execution has led many experts to believe he was killed in a ritual sacrifice.

The archaeological evidence that the Celts practiced human sacrifice is to some extent backed up by references in classical literature. For example, the Greek writer Strabo (c. 64 B.C.E.–24 C.E.) said the Celts used several methods of

Left: The remains of Lindow Man were found in the boggy ground of Lindow Moss in northern England. Bogs are cold, acidic, and exclude air and sunlight, making them the ideal habitat for preserving bodies and other objects.

human sacrifice. It was carried out by their priests, the druids. Victims might be shot with arrows or impaled on sharp stakes of wood. Sometimes they were placed within large wickerwork frames in the shape of human figures, which were set on fire.

The Face of Lindow Man
Scientists have been able to reconstruct the face of Lindow Man from his 2,000-year-old skull. Their efforts show him to have had deep-set eyes and a beard. Experts believe he stood 5 ft 7 in (1.7 m) tall.

Above: The head and torso of Lindow Man emerge from the soil. Archaeologists found traces of bread in his stomach, suggesting that he had eaten a ritual meal before he died. They also found pollen from the mistletoe plant, which was sacred to the druids.

THE DEATH OF CUCHULAINN

Soon after the Cattle Raid of Cooley had come to a bloody end, Queen Medb of Connacht decided to wreak her revenge on Cuchulainn, who had slaughtered so many of her men. In order to ensnare and kill him, the queen asked for help from the evil children of Calitin. Calitin was a sorcerer and his children had learned their black arts at the hands of druids.

The children soon set about their deadly work and tried to lure Cuchulainn away from his stronghold. To do this they created the illusion of an invading Connacht army by whipping up leaves and thistles and transforming them into troops. For two days Cuchulainn fought these phantom soldiers until he was exhausted. Eventually, his friends convinced him he was being fooled by sorcery and urged him to take refuge in a secluded valley to escape the tricks of his enemies. But Cuchulainn still could not avoid the children. They discovered his hiding place and again filled the countryside with the sights and sounds of battle: trumpets, shouts, wailing, and loud screams. Soon Cuchulainn could bear it no longer and set out to do battle with Medb's forces single-handed.

BAD OMENS

Before he fought Medb's men, however, Cuchulainn experienced a number of omens, or frightening signs, that seemed to point toward his coming death. First his horse, the Gray of Macha, galloped away from him and, when it was caught, it shed tears of blood. Then his weapons clattered down by his feet as he was riding in his chariot. Next, three women sitting by the roadside offered him a portion of dog meat. Although he was forbidden from eating dog meat by sacred law, he was also obliged by the rules of hospitality to accept it. After eating the meat, he felt his strength draining from his body. Finally, when he came to a ford, he saw a young woman, weeping and wailing, and washing blood-stained clothes in the water, turning it red. He knew instinctively that these were his clothes and that his death was being symbolically enacted.

Undaunted by these omens, Cuchulainn drove on and finally came to a hill called Slieve Fuad in present-day Armagh, where he found Medb's real, human army ready to meet him. In a brief battle, Cuchulainn slaughtered hundreds of Medb's forces. This convinced the Connacht men, led by Lugaid (lewy) and Erc, that they had to resort to trickery.

A TRICK

With Cuchulainn again about to enter the fray, a druid, urged on by Lugaid, demanded that the Ulsterman give him his spear, knowing that Cuchulainn was bound by honor not to refuse him. Cuchulainn agreed to the request, but flung the spear so hard that it not only killed the druid but also nine men standing behind him. However, Lugaid was able to get his hands on the precious spear and he hurled it back, killing Cuchulainn's charioteer, Laeg (loyg).

The Connacht men then repeated the trick: another druid demanded the spear—and paid the price with his life when Cuchulainn hurled it at him. This time Erc picked up the weapon and threw it back, fatally wounding the Gray of Macha. When the same sequence of events happened a third time, it was Cuchulainn himself who was struck by his own weapon.

Bleeding from his wound, Cuchulainn dragged himself from the battlefield to a nearby lake. He knew he was dying. By the lake he found a tall pillar stone to which he tied himself with his belt, wanting to end his days standing up like a hero.

The Connacht men had followed the wounded hero. At first they were afraid to come too near as they could still see his warrior light shining above his head. But when Lugaid finally picked up the courage to move in and decapitate the failing Ulster hero, the stricken Gray of Macha suddenly appeared and charged at his master's enemies, scattering them, before trotting away to die.

The Connacht men kept watch over Cuchulainn from a safe distance. After three days the war god, Morrigan, in the guise of a raven, landed on his shoulder. This was a

Left: The death of Cuchulainn is depicted in this powerful sculpture in the General Post Office in Dublin. It shows the hero tied to a stone, with the god Morrigan, in the form of a raven, on his shoulder.

THE DRUIDS

Druids often appear in Celtic myths, in which they are described as being wise and the workers of magic. The druids were the priests of the ancient Celts. Most of what is known about them comes from Roman writers. There were three types of druids: prophets, bards (poets), and priests. They were expert in astrology, divination (foretelling the future), and healing with herbs. They held the oak and mistletoe sacred, and performed rites and rituals in forests.

The druids were keepers of the tribe's traditions. They spent years memorizing laws, history, and poetry. They presided at festivals and sacrifices, which may have included human sacrifices, and they also acted as judges in disputes.

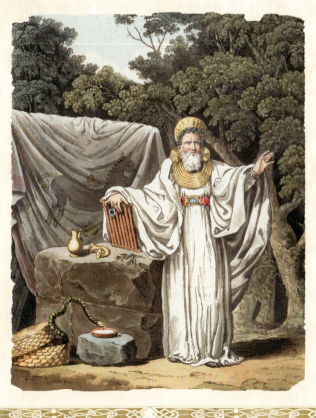

Right: Dressed in ceremonial robes, a druid raises his right hand—perhaps to pronounce a judgement—in this fanciful early nineteenth-century illustration.

sign that death was near. The men watched as Cuchulainn's warrior light faded to nothing. Lugaid stepped forward and cut off the dead Cuchulainn's head—but as he did so he dislodged the hero's sword from his hand and this sliced through Lugaid's own wrist. Cuchulainn's head was then taken off to Tara to be buried. His headless corpse was left bound to the stone. As was predicted at his birth, Cuchulainn's life had been short, but his fame would live for evermore.

The Hill of Tara in County Meath was the home of the High Kings of Ireland and is one of the country's most famous sites. Seen here are the remains of Tara's two ring forts inside a circular enclosure.

Heroes of the Fianna

The Fenian Cycle is the third traditional group of Irish myths. It focuses on the daring deeds of an elite Irish war band known as the Fianna. The cycle's stories feature the heroic Finn Mac Cumhaill (fin mac-cool), who became leader of the Fianna during the reign of the Irish king Conn of the Hundred Battles.

Finn and his men, who included his son Oisin (usheen) and his friend Diarmuid (deermud), had many adventures while protecting Ireland from its foes. When they were not fighting, they spent their time hunting and feasting. They also encountered inhabitants of the Otherworld, and Oisin even went to live in this other realm. When he returned to Ireland, he did not at first realize that 300 years had passed and all his family and friends had long since died.

FINN SAVES TARA

The Fianna were an elite group of warriors who served the Irish king. Their leader was the brave Cumhaill, until he was killed in a battle against other Irishmen. On Cumhaill's death, leadership of the Fianna passed to his rival, Goll. Goll was frightened that Cumhaill's young son, Finn, would eventually try to take revenge and make himself head of the Fianna.

The young Finn grew up in grave danger of being killed by Goll. He had to be careful to hide from Goll's men, so he lived deep in the countryside, cut off from the world of warriors. Eventually Finn made contact with an uncle, who enthralled him with stories of the Fianna and the bravery of his father. This made Finn determined to defeat Goll and win the leadership of the Fianna.

Although he was already a skilled hunter and fighter, Finn needed to learn the art of poetry if he was to gain the respect of his fellow fighters. He set off in search of a wise old teacher named Finnegas, who, for seven years, had been living near a river in the hope of catching the Salmon of Knowledge. This was a magical fish that would impart wisdom and knowledge to whoever ate it. Soon after Finn found Finnegas, the old man caught the Salmon and gave it to Finn to cook. As Finn was grilling the fish, he touched it and burned his thumb. He stuck his thumb into his mouth and was immediately granted knowledge. Finnegas then gave Finn the whole fish to eat, and in this way Finn was granted eternal wisdom.

Goll's fears about Finn seemed to be well founded when, one day, Finn walked into the court of the Irish king, Conn of the Hundred Battles, at Tara. It was the time of a great six-week festival, when all fighting was outlawed. When Conn saw this young stranger in their midst, he asked him who he was. Finn replied that he was the son of Cumhaill, former leader of the Fianna, and that he had come to do service for the king. Conn, who had fond memories of Finn's father, welcomed him to his court, and Finn swore an oath of allegiance to him.

HUNTING AND FARMING

Like Finn Mac Cumhaill and the Fianna, the ancient Celts enjoyed hunting. They hunted mainly to kill pests and predators and for animal skins, which they used for clothing. Hunters would use slings and bows and arrows to shoot their prey, and hunting dogs were specially bred for the chase. Among the animals the Celts hunted were boar, deer, wolves, and foxes.

However, the Celts spent most of their time not hunting but farming. They kept pigs, cattle, sheep (which also provided wool), and horses, which were bred for hunting and war. In the fields, Celtic farmers grew wheat, barley, and millet. Other foods included peas, beans, and lentils. Along with nuts and berries from woodlands, these foods gave the Celts a relatively well-balanced and healthy diet.

Below: Butser Farm in Hampshire, southern England, was set up as a reconstruction of a Celtic settlement in 1972. Celtic building methods and materials were replicated as closely as possible, and fields, such as this one, were sown with crops that existed in Celtic times.

Celtic Myth

THE DEMON AND THE MAGIC SPEAR

Shortly after Finn's arrival, the king warned everyone that the time was approaching when an evil demon named Aillen would come to Tara and set fire to it. The demon did this every year on a certain night. He came at dusk and put everyone to sleep with his beautiful harp music, and then he blasted the royal buildings with fire from his mouth.

Conn was desperate to find someone to defeat Aillen. When Finn heard about this, he asked the king if he could fight the demon. The king readily agreed and swore that if Finn succeeded he would take Goll's place as leader of the Fianna.

Before the demon arrived, Finn was given a magical spear by one of his father's old friends. This man told Finn that the spear always hit its target. And, crucially, if Finn held the spear against his head when Aillen was playing his music, he would not fall asleep.

On the night the demon was due to come, Finn went outside the walls of Tara to await him. Soon he could hear a strange, unearthly music. Aillen was approaching, playing his instrument. While all the Irishmen inside Tara fell asleep, Finn touched his head with his magic spear and remained awake. The demon, thinking everyone was asleep, got ready to burn down Tara. But then, to his horror, he saw Finn facing him. He realized that the spell cast by his music had failed and ran away as fast as he could to his home on the top of a mountain. Quick as lightning, Finn sped after the demon and threw the magic spear at him. The weapon killed the demon with one strike, and then Finn cut off the corpse's head. He brought the head back to Tara as proof of his victory.

Next day, when Conn and his men awoke from the spell, they found that Tara had not been burned. Filled with joy and relief, they rushed outside and saw the head of Aillen, with Finn standing next to it. The king remembered the promise he had given Finn. He called over Goll and told him that he either had to let Finn lead the Fianna and swear allegiance to him or else leave the country. Goll decided to fight under Finn. So Finn became captain of the Fianna, just as his father had been before him.

Opposite: The hero Finn Mac Cumhaill stands ready to do battle with the demon Aillen in this early twentieth-century illustration. Finn is holding the magical spear that prevented him from falling asleep to Aillen's hypnotic music.

DIARMUID AND GRÁINNE

Many years after his wife died, Finn Mac Cumhaill—now an old man—grew increasingly sad and lonely. So the famous leader of the Fianna decided that he should remarry. The woman he chose as his bride was Gráinne (gronya), King Cormac of Ireland's daughter and the most beautiful girl in the country. Ireland's greatest nobles went to Cormac's palace at Tara for the wedding.

Gráinne did not meet her husband-to-be until the wedding day. And when she finally set eyes on Finn, her heart sank. He was old enough to be her grandfather! After the ceremony, there was a splendid feast, but Gráinne could barely eat a thing. When she looked miserably around the great hall, she noticed all the young Fianna warriors. Why couldn't she have a young husband instead? She asked one of her father's druids to tell her the names of the Fianna warriors. The two she thought were most handsome were called Oisin—Finn's own son—and Diarmuid.

On a wicked impulse, Gráinne decided there and then that she had to run away with one of these two men. First she approached Oisin. He was flattered and tempted by her beauty, but told her he would never betray his father. Gráinne then turned her charms on Diarmuid. He, too, refused to betray Finn, who was not only his leader but his friend. But Gráinne was determined to get her way. She imposed a *geis* (gesh)—a solemn, sacred bond—on Diarmuid. This *geis* was a promise that he would run away with her.

Even though the promise had been forced on him against his will, Diarmuid knew that to break it meant losing his honor. This was unthinkable for a Fianna warrior. Yet how could he treat Finn so cruelly? He begged Gráinne to release him from her bond, but she refused. He asked his closest friends what they thought he should do. They all reluctantly agreed that he should escape from Tara with Gráinne rather than break the *geis*.

Left: Many prehistoric stone monuments in Ireland are known as "Diarmuid and Gráinne's Bed," commemorating the journey of the fleeing lovers. This "bed" is Kilclooney Dolmen in County Donegal. It consists of two upright slabs supporting a huge capstone, measuring about 13 by 20 ft (4 by 6 m).

FINN'S FURY

The following night, Gráinne and Diarmuid crept out of the palace. They stole Finn's chariot and horses, and drove west to Athlone. There, knowing that Finn would soon be on their trail, they abandoned the vehicle and slipped into the woods. Back at Tara, Finn awoke to find his young wife missing—and soon discovered that Diarmuid had gone, too. He exploded with anger, and rushed out with his band of warriors to track the fugitives down. Finn kept hard on the heels of the couple, but they always remained just beyond his grasp.

One time, when Diarmuid realized Finn was getting near, he built a wooden stockade. Finn surrounded this hideout and positioned guards at each of its seven exits. Now, he thought, he was sure to capture the runaways. But the god Aengus Og came to the rescue and spirited Gráinne away to another wood. Then Diarmuid pole-vaulted over the door where Finn himself was standing guard and ran off to join Gráinne.

And so the chase continued, month after month. Finn hired mercenary soldiers from across the waters to kill Diarmuid, but the young hero defeated them and tied them up.

Above: The mountain of Ben Bulben rises from the plains of present-day County Sligo in northwest Ireland. It was on the slopes of Ben Bulben that Diarmuid met his death.

He overcame two warriors of the Morna clan, sent by Finn. And he also killed a giant, who was guarding some magical berries that Gráinne wanted to eat. On another occasion, he and Gráinne were taking refuge up a tree when Finn and his men surrounded it. Again, just when it seemed capture was inevitable, Aengus Og spirited Gráinne away, and Diarmuid leapt over the heads of his attackers and escaped.

Eventually, after sixteen years of chasing, Finn grew weary and agreed to make peace with Diarmuid. The couple went off to live together and they had four sons and a daughter. In time, Gráinne decided to invite her father and Finn to their home for a feast. The former enemies drank and ate together, and the banquet lasted a whole year.

A FATEFUL HUNT

Finn had never forgiven Diarmuid. One day, when they were hunting on the slopes of Ben Bulben, Finn encouraged Diarmuid to fight a large, magical boar that had caused the other hunters to flee. Diarmuid accepted the challenge, but the boar was too powerful and dealt him terrible wounds. As he lay dying, Diarmuid begged Finn to bring him some water, knowing that he would be healed by water that had touched Finn's hands. But Finn refused.

Gráinne was distraught when she learned of her husband's death, and she vowed that her children would take vengeance on Finn. But over the succeeding months, Finn visited her and managed to calm her down—and eventually gain her favor. Finally, she even consented to be his wife. Gráinne then persuaded her children to forgive her new husband, as she herself had done, and Finn promised them places among the ranks of the Fianna.

Right: Diarmuid died after being savaged by a boar on Ben Bulben. The Celts revered the boar and celebrated it in their art. This bronze boar was found in Loiret in France and dates from the first century C.E.

BURYING THE DEAD

The manner in which the Celts disposed of their dead varied according to time and place. Before 400 B.C.E., for example, people were often buried under earthen mounds, or barrows. After this date, it became more common to lay the dead to rest in level graves without mounds.

The Celts believed that the soul survived the body after death, and so it was important to provide the deceased with objects that could be taken to the afterlife. Celtic nobles were laid to rest with their clothes on, and given food and drink. Some of them were buried with a wagon or a chariot. The Celtic chieftain from the sixth century B.C.E. who was unearthed at Hochdorf in Germany, for example, was accompanied by a four-wheeled cart bearing various goods, including a spear, axe, and horse harness.

The Celts also cremated bodies. During Roman times, bodies were burned and the ashes collected and buried in a grave along with drinking vessels and portions of food, such as pork.

Celtic Art

Alongside their myths and legends, the greatest legacy of the Celts is their art. Celtic craftspeople were skilled metal workers, creating fine shields, swords, and jewelry. Artists used metals found in their own lands, including tin and copper. They also imported materials from abroad, such as amber from the Baltic and coral from the Mediterranean.

This elegant gold torc, or neck ring, was found in a grave at Waldalgesheim in Germany. Its ends, or finials, are decorated with patterns of curving lines, typical of the La Tène style.

PRE-CHRISTIAN ART

The most famous style of Celtic art is called La Tène, after an archaeological site in Switzerland. This style lasted from about the fifth to the first century B.C.E. It features animals, human figures, and the curving, interlocking lines of leaves and branches.

Left: This bronze plaque, with its swirling shapes, was probably part of a horse's harness. It is decorated with enamel, which is a thin layer of glass, colored by minerals, and applied to the metal.

CHRISTIAN ART IN IRELAND

Ireland was converted to Christianity in the fifth century C.E., largely due to the efforts of St. Patrick. Irish craftspeople continued to use the curving, weaving lines of pre-Christian Celtic art, but now the centers of artistic creation were the monasteries. Here the monks produced beautiful metalwork such as chalices (cups to hold wine during the Communion service), stone crosses, and illuminated (illustrated) manuscripts.

The finest of these manuscripts is the *Book of Kells*, named after the monastery in County Meath that housed it for several hundred years. It is now displayed in Trinity College, Dublin. Most scholars believe the book was begun, if not finished, at the Irish monastery of Iona off the west coast of Scotland in the late eighth century C.E.

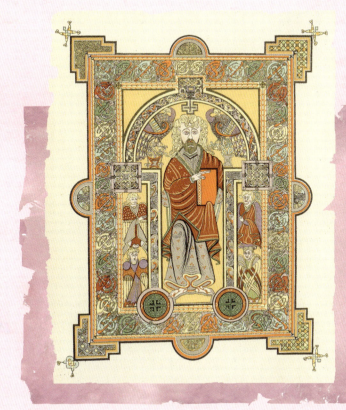

Above: The Ardagh Chalice was created in Ireland in the eighth century C.E. It is made of silver, brass, bronze, and enamel. Although intended for use in a Christian church, the chalice displays traditional pagan Celtic designs in its curving, interlocking lines. The chalice was found in 1868 by two boys digging for potatoes near Ardagh, County Limerick.

Left: St. Matthew holds a copy of his gospel in this illumination from the *Book of Kells*. The book presents the four gospels of the Bible's New Testament and its illuminations show biblical stories alongside abstract designs. The illuminators used a range of natural colors, such as green from treated copper and blue from lapis lazuli.

OISIN AND THE
LAND OF YOUTH

Finn, his sons, and the Fianna warriors were enjoying themselves hunting near Lough Leane in County Kerry. As they rested in the woods, they saw a woman riding toward them on a white horse. She was young and beautiful, dressed like a princess, with a golden crown on her golden hair. She rode up to Finn and his men and told them she was looking for Oisin, Finn's son.

Oisin was astonished to hear his name being spoken by this enchanting woman. He was even more amazed when the woman said she loved him so much she wanted to take him back home. She told them her name was Niamh (neave) of the Golden Hair, and that she lived in the Land of Youth across the seas. It was a place, she said, where no one grew old or sick. Trees and flowers blossomed all the year round, and wine and honey never ran out. She said Oisin would live in a splendid palace and have sturdy horses and swift hounds to hunt with. And they would both live together in perfect happiness.

Oisin was spellbound by her words and readily agreed to go with her. He climbed onto her horse, put his arms round her waist, and said goodbye to his father. Finn was sad because in his heart he knew he would not see his son again.

A LIFE OF LUXURY

So Niamh and Oisin set off across the waters toward the Land of Youth. Along the way they saw marvelous palaces, towers, and castles, as well as many strange creatures. One time, a young woman rode past them on a brown horse, clutching a golden apple. Chasing her on a white horse was a handsome young man, his red cloak flowing in the breeze. He was holding a golden sword. When Oisin asked Niamh what these strange sights meant, she told him not to ask such questions.

Above: The banks of Lough Leane in County Kerry were the setting for Oisin's meeting with Niamh.

THE CELTIC CALENDAR

The Celts were very aware of the passage of time and had their own calendar. They based it on observations of the moon and counted nights rather than days.

The Celts marked the year with four main festivals. The new year began in the fall on the festival of Samhain (sowin) on November 1. This was the time when the boundaries with the Other world dissolved and the dead might return to the land of the living. The festival of Halloween is based on Samhain.

The festival of Imbolc, on February 1, was linked with the birth of lambs. Beltaine (bell-tinner), on May 1, celebrated fire, the sun's spring warmth, and the fertility of crops. Cattle were let loose into the fields and driven between two fires to safeguard them from disease. The last festival, Lughnasa (lew-nassa), took place throughout July and August. It was associated with the god Lugh and with the harvest.

Right: This Celtic calendar, inscribed on a bronze plate, was found at Coligny in France. Although the numbers and letters are in Latin, the language is that of the Celts of Gaul. Months were reckoned by fortnights rather than weeks, and days were marked "good" or "bad."

72   Celtic Myth

Eventually, the young couple arrived in the Land of Youth, where they were welcomed by crowds of people. Just as Niamh had described it, the place was like paradise. She took Oisin to her palace, and they lived there in great luxury, with hundreds of servants ready to meet their every need.

Oisin was enchanted by the Land of Youth and blissfully happy to have Niamh as his wife. But in time he began to miss his old life in Ireland. He thought of his father and the happy days hunting with his friends. Despite the wonderful luxuries he was enjoying, he grew homesick. One day he told Niamh that he wanted to return home to see his family and friends. Niamh was horrified at this, for she feared he would never return. She begged him not to go, but Oisin insisted. Finally Niamh gave him her permission, but she warned him that he must never touch the soil of Ireland with his foot. If he did, he would never come back.

THE RETURN TO IRELAND

Setting out from the Land of Youth on horseback, Oisin crossed the seas and soon saw the coastline of his beloved country once again. But he did not realize that 300 years had passed since he had left home. Not only that, but a new religion had reached Ireland. St. Patrick had arrived and was converting the Irish to Christianity.

As Oisin rode across the land, he noticed that the people were much smaller than he had remembered. He asked some of them where Finn Mac Cumhaill was, and was told that Finn had died centuries ago. With great sorrow in his heart, Oisin realized that all his family and friends had perished. He journeyed to the Hill of Allen in Kildare to see his father's old home. But when he arrived he found only grassy mounds.

He then rode to the Valley of Thrushes in Wicklow. There he saw a crowd of people trying in vain to lift a large slab of stone. Taking pity on their feebleness, he rode up to them, leaned over from his horse, and easily lifted the stone. But as he did so, his saddle strap snapped and he tumbled to the earth. What Niamh feared had come to pass, and a ghastly transformation took place. The tall, handsome warrior turned into a shrunken, wizened old man.

The crowd was shocked and asked Oisin who he was. Oisin told them his story, and they thought it best to take him to St. Patrick himself. Oisin did not have long to live. But he did manage to meet St. Patrick, who listened to his strange tale and had it written down to preserve it for future generations.

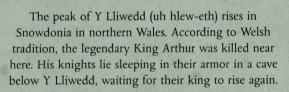

The peak of Y Lliwedd (uh hlew-eth) rises in Snowdonia in northern Wales. According to Welsh tradition, the legendary King Arthur was killed near here. His knights lie sleeping in their armor in a cave below Y Lliwedd, waiting for their king to rise again.

Myths of the Welsh

The collection of eleven stories known as the *Mabinogion* is the greatest treasury of Welsh myths and legends. The tales were recorded in two medieval manuscripts dating from the fourteenth century, but they are based on much older stories. The first full translation into English was made by Lady Charlotte Guest in 1838.

The stories of the *Mabinogion* describe quests, battles, love affairs, and encounters with the supernatural. They mix legendary with semi-historical characters. Heroes include Pwyll (poo-ihl), lord of Dyfed (duh-ved), who swapped places with the king of the Otherworld for a year, and the giant Bran, who, in Welsh mythology, was King of the Britons. Bran went to war with the Irish to avenge the maltreatment of his sister, who had married the Irish king. Other tales mention Arthur, the famous legendary British king. In one of the stories, Arthur helps his cousin, the young hero Culhwch (culhuc), to set out on a quest to marry Olwen, the beautiful daughter of a dangerous giant.

PRINCE PWYLL IN THE
OTHERWORLD

One day, Prince Pwyll of Dyfed, in southwest Wales, was out hunting with his pack of hounds when he saw another hunter's pack attacking a stag. These other hounds were strange in appearance. Their coats were glowing white, but their ears were bright red. Pwyll drove them off with his own hounds and was about to catch the stag when an imposing horseman approached him.

The rider was strong and noble-looking, dressed for the hunt entirely in gray and riding a gray horse. He turned out to be Arawn, a king in Annwn, the Welsh Otherworld. He was angry with Pwyll for driving his hounds away and accused the prince of rude behavior. Pwyll accepted that he was in the wrong and apologized to the Otherworld king. He asked if he could make amends in any way.

Arawn replied that there was a favor Pwyll could do for him. He told the prince that in the Otherworld he was at war with a rival king named Hafgan. He asked Pwyll to live in the Otherworld for a year and at the end of that time to fight Hafgan in a duel.

Arawn said he would make Pwyll look exactly like himself, so that all his people would believe that it was still Arawn who was ruling over them. At the same time Arawn acknowledged that it would be unfair to deprive Pwyll's people of their king for so long. So Arawn would make himself look like Pwyll and promised to rule over the kingdom of Dyfed wisely and generously. In a year and a day's time they would meet again at the same spot. Arawn also told Pwyll what to do when he fought Hafgan. He must kill him with a single stroke of his weapon. He must not strike him with a second blow. If he did so, Hafgan would regain all his strength.

THE EISTEDDFOD FESTIVAL

The modern Welsh language evolved from an ancient Celtic tongue, and the tradition of writing poetry and prose in Welsh is still honored at the annual National Eisteddfod Festival. Derived from the Welsh word for "sitting," the Eisteddfod (ay-steth-vod) can be traced back to 1176, when Lord Rhys of Cardigan invited musicians and poets to perform at his castle. Over the centuries this festival tradition continued and it was formalized in 1880 with the founding of a national association.

During this annual festival, presentations are made to the best poets and writers in Welsh. These ceremonies are presided over by the Archdruid, who is head of the Gorsedd of Bards, an organization that honors Welsh writers, musicians, and artists. Alongside the formal ceremonies, there are also many stalls selling Welsh books, crafts, and food, and tents for Welsh language learners and for live music.

In this way, the Eisteddfod helps to nurture the Welsh people's pride in their Celtic past.

Right: Dressed in impressive robes, the Archdruid performs rituals and duties at the Eisteddfod. Here he is presented with the symbolic Horn of Plenty by a local woman.

A YEAR IN ANNWN

Pwyll agreed to Arawn's request and set off to Annwn—looking and sounding just like Arawn. He made himself at home in the king's palace and was delighted by all the luxuries he found there. Food was served on golden dishes, there were silk clothes to wear, and there was a beautiful queen for his wife.

For a whole year Pwyll ruled in Annwn, feasting, hunting, and enjoying good company. But he never dared hold or kiss his lovely queen, for fear of insulting Arawn. The queen, who did not suspect that her husband was really Pwyll, wondered why he seemed to be so cold toward her. But she accepted his behavior.

Soon the year was up and Pwyll got ready to fight King Hafgan. He rode out to a ford in a river and waited for his enemy to come. Sure enough, Hafgan arrived and the two men began to fight.

Pwyll immediately gained an advantage and struck Hafgan's shield so hard that the blow split both the shield and the king's armor. As he hung from his horse, Hafgan knew he had been fatally wounded and begged Pwyll to finish him off with a second deadly blow.

But remembering Arawn's instructions, Pwyll refused, and Hafgan's nobles took their king off to die. Within a day, Pwyll established his rule over Hafgan's country and had united Annwn.

THE KINGS RETURN

With his mission accomplished, Pwyll set out to meet Arawn, as they had arranged. Arawn was delighted to hear that Hafgan had been killed and thanked the prince. The two men then regained their old appearances and returned to their own kingdoms.

Arawn was pleased to be back home and spent his first day feasting. That night, when he came to kiss his wife, he was surprised to find her withdrawn and silent. When he asked her what the matter was, she told him that since he had ignored her for a year she was now taken aback to receive his warmth and love. Arawn realized that Pwyll had been very honorable and had not touched his wife for the whole year. He then told his wife the whole story.

Meanwhile, Pwyll returned to Dyfed and summoned all his lords. He asked them how they thought he had ruled over them for the past year. They told him that he had been a most just, wise, and generous ruler. Pwyll was grateful that Arawn had governed his people so well, and he told them exactly what had happened.

Pwyll and Arawn continued their friendship over the years that followed. They would send each other presents of jewels, armor, hawks, horses, and greyhounds. And, in recognition of his successful year's reign in the Otherworld, Pwyll was renamed Prince Pwyll of Annwn.

Left: The Celts enjoyed hunting deer, as the story of Pwyll suggests. This bronze figure of a stag was made in Gaul and dates from the first century B.C.E.

Branwen's Marriage

> Bran the Blessed, the giant king of the Britons, was sitting on a rock by the sea in his kingdom of Harlech, when he saw thirteen ships sailing toward the shoreline. Bran wondered who these strangers were. Very soon the vessels landed and out stepped Matholwch (matholaw), king of Ireland, and his men. When asked what he wanted, Matholwch declared that he sought an alliance with the Britons and desired to marry the beautiful Branwen, Bran's sister.

Bran accepted the king's offer and began to make preparations for a splendid wedding that would unite the peoples of Britain and Ireland. The marriage duly took place, and Matholwch was delighted with his bride. Everything was going well until Bran's half-brother, Efnisien, turned up. Efnisien was absolutely furious that he had not been consulted about the marriage. He was a troublemaker by nature, and now he took out his rage and spite on the Irish king's horses, cruelly cutting off their lips, ears, tails, and eyelids.

When Matholwch was told about this atrocity, he was so shocked that he decided to return home immediately. Bran was outraged, too, and tried to make amends for his half-brother's crime. He offered to replace Matholwch's horses and to give him gold and silver, as well as a huge magic cauldron that brought the dead back to life when they were thrown into it.

Matholwch accepted the offer and in due course sailed back home with his new wife. In Ireland, Branwen was at first received with great joy and warmth by the people. She and her husband soon had a son, named Gwern. But in time the story of how Efnisien had insulted Matholwch became known, and the Irish began to feel resentful toward Branwen. They persuaded the king to make her toil in the kitchens, where the royal butcher would box her ears. They prevented ships from leaving for Britain and imprisoned British visitors so that Bran would not hear of his sister's mistreatment.

But Branwen wrote a letter describing her miserable treatment and attached it to a tame starling. She sent the bird off to Harlech, where it landed on Bran's shoulder. The king read the letter and was outraged. He set about gathering together a large fleet to invade Ireland and rescue his sister.

TWO KINGDOMS GO TO WAR

When the Irish saw the approaching British ships, they were so shaken by the size of the invasion force that they quickly made a plan. They decided to build a huge hall—large enough to fit the giant Bran—and to offer to let Gwern, Branwen's son, rule the Irish kingdom instead of Matholwch. But the Irish also had a trick up their sleeves. They planned to hide two hundred soldiers inside flour bags and hang them on the pillars of the hall's walls. When the signal was given, they would jump out and ambush the Britons.

Right: This bronze leaf shows a Celtic woman wearing a long, patterned dress and boots, such as a well-born Celtic lady like Branwen might have worn.

CELTIC HEADHUNTING

The cutting off of Bran's head is a reminder of how much value the Celts put on this part of the body. According to the Greek historian Diodorus Siculus (c. 90–30 B.C.E.), Celtic warriors used to cut off the heads of their enemies on the battlefield. They would then nail the heads to the walls of their houses or keep those of important foes pickled in oil in a chest. Other sources say that they hung severed heads from their horses' saddles or stuck them onto the points of spears.

The Romans found Celtic headhunting extremely shocking. But for the Celts, the head was where a person's soul lived. By cutting off a head, they made sure that both body and soul had perished and the enemy was well and truly dead. The Celts also placed human heads in shrines, such as the sixth-century B.C.E. sanctuary of Roquepertuse in France, possibly as offerings to the gods.

Right: Skulls of young men were set into the portico of the Celtic sanctuary of Roquepertuse in Provence, France. The skulls may have belonged to warriors who died in battle and were being offered to the gods.

When Bran and his men landed on Irish soil, they agreed to the terms offered by Matholwch and proceeded to the newly built hall for a celebration feast. The banquet was soon under way and Gwern was declared ruler of Ireland. Then, in a sudden fit of blind, senseless rage, Efnisien picked up the young Gwern and threw him into the great hearth fire. Immediately there were shouts and screams as the Irish leaped from the flour bags. The Britons unsheathed their weapons, and both sides surged into the fray.

The fight continued day after day. But the Irish had the magic cauldron, and the dead soldiers they threw into it at night came back to life the next morning. The situation seemed hopeless for the Britons until Efnisien got himself thrown into the cauldron by posing as a dead Irish soldier. Once in the vessel he stretched himself out and managed to break it into four pieces, killing himself in the process.

The Britons still had the worst of the battle. Bran was fatally wounded with a poisoned arrow, and only seven other British warriors remained standing by the end. The dying Bran ordered them to cut off his head and take it to the White Mount in London. He said they should first take his head to Harlech and stop there for seven years, then go on to Pembroke, where they should stay for eighty years. Only then were they to proceed to London.

So the seven Britons left for Harlech, carrying Bran's head with them. Branwen went too, but when she arrived home she

Above: The head of Bran is carried back from Ireland by his Welsh followers in this modern illustration by Alan Lee. The head is said to have found its final resting place in London.

felt so sorry that she had caused the destruction of two countries that her heart broke and she died. The soldiers continued their journey, and all the time they were in Harlech and Pembroke Bran's head talked to them, encouraging and advising them. Finally, they brought it to London, where they buried it according to Bran's instructions.

The Gundestrup Cauldron

In many Celtic myths and legends, cauldrons are depicted as sacred objects. In Irish tales, they are found in the hostels of the Otherworld, providing an inexhaustible supply of food. And in the Welsh story of Branwen's Marriage, the Irish king Matholwch possesses a magic cauldron that brings the dead to life.

SACRED VESSELS

The ancient Celts used cauldrons for heating liquids and cooking foods. They also buried them in lakes and bogs, possibly as gifts to the gods. The most magnificent of these sacred vessels is the Gundestrup Cauldron. It was made in the second or first century B.C.E., possibly in Thrace (present-day Bulgaria).

Below: Horsemen and foot soldiers march in a procession in this detail from one of the cauldron's panels. The soldiers wear shorts and carry rectangular shields. The figures on the right are blowing boar-headed trumpets.

Left: A bearded man, his two arms raised, looms from the outside of the cauldron. The vessel, which can hold nearly thirty gallons (110 liters) of liquid, was not made in one piece but as a series of plates that were dismantled before the vessel was concealed in marshy ground. Scholars believe it was a votary offering to the gods—a gift to gain their help or approval.

Left: In a scene from the cauldron, a giant man wearing a close-fitting cap holds a smaller man over a cauldron, bucket, or similar vessel. The scene may show a human sacrifice by ritual drowning. Alternatively, the giant may be about to dip a dead soldier in a vessel of immortality, as in the story of Branwen.

Below: The base of the cauldron shows the ritual killing of a bull. A hound lies dead under the bull's hooves, while a warrior is poised to stab the beast through the neck.

The cauldron was found in 1891 in a bog near the hamlet of Gundestrup in northern Jutland, Denmark. How the cauldron got from southeastern to northern Europe is not known for sure. It may have been taken there as war booty by a Germanic tribe. Because it was made of new silver, scholars believe that it was intended for a religious ceremony rather than for cooking.

The wonder of the cauldron is the series of figures portrayed on the silver plates. These provide a fascinating window onto the world of Celtic myth and everyday Celtic life. The figures range from a ram-horned snake and catlike creatures to gods and soldiers.

CULHWCH AND OLWEN

Shortly after Culhwch was born, his mother fell ill and died. His father, King Celyddon, eventually got over his grief and remarried. The king's new wife thought that Culhwch was a handsome young man and wanted him to marry her daughter by a previous husband. Culhwch hesitated over this suggestion, whereupon his stepmother took deep offense and prophesied that the only woman he would marry would be Olwen, the beautiful daughter of a frightening giant called Ysbaddaden (usbath-adden).

When Culhwch's father heard about his wife's prophecy, he advised his son to go to the court of King Arthur for help. Arthur was Culhwch's cousin and was happy to be of assistance. Arthur had never heard of the lovely Olwen, but he arranged for some of his knights to accompany Culhwch on his quest to find her. These knights included Cei (kay), who could hold his breath under water for nine days and nine nights, and Bedwyr, who had only one arm but was as powerful as three soldiers nevertheless.

Culhwch and his fellow warriors set off from Arthur's castle and journeyed over mountains and through valleys. Eventually they came to a vast plain. At the end of it loomed a gigantic castle, which seemed to the warriors to be the loveliest castle in the world. They rode toward it for three days, but the plain was so huge that they were scarcely any nearer to the castle. On the third day they came across a herdsman and his wife, who told them that the castle belonged to Ysbaddaden. When the herdsman heard they were seeking Olwen, the giant's daughter, he tried to warn them off. The giant, he explained, had killed many young men wanting to marry his daughter. The herdsman's wife added that the giant had killed all but one of their twenty-four sons. She revealed that Olwen came to their cottage to wash her hair once a week, and told Culhwch that he could see her then if he wanted to.

Left: Olwen, shown here in a painting by Alan Lee, agreed to marry Culhwch only if her father, the giant Ysbaddaden, agreed to the match.

Culhwch waited for Olwen at the cottage. When she came, he was astounded by her beauty. She had golden hair and snow-white skin, and was wearing a flame-red dress. Culhwch told her immediately that he was in love with her and wanted to marry her.

Olwen was fascinated by this handsome young prince, but said she could only marry him if her father, Ysbaddaden, agreed to it. She told Culhwch that her father would make him perform a series of nearly impossible tasks before he would give his consent.

THE GIANT'S LABORS

The knights went straight to the castle and met Ysbaddaden. Culhwch declared that he wanted to marry his daughter, and the giant replied that Culhwch must carry out a long list of labors. These included finding a missing hunter named Mabon, son of Modron, and, hardest of all, bringing him the razor, comb, and shears that lay between the ears of a ferocious wild boar named Twrch Trwyth (toorch trooeth). Ysbaddaden said that only those implements were strong and sharp enough to cut his beard: if Culhwch brought them back, Olwen would be his wife.

Culhwch and his companions rode off to tackle the giant's tasks. When it came to finding Mabon, they asked for the help of several animals, including a stag, an owl, and an eagle. Finally, a salmon revealed that Mabon was imprisoned in a castle in Gloucester in England. Culhwch and his men returned to Arthur's court to get reinforcements. With a huge army, Culhwch and Arthur besieged the fortress and rescued Mabon, who escaped down the river on the back of the salmon.

The knights then turned their attention to the boar, Twrch Trwyth. The creature was living in Ireland, and Arthur sent a large force to capture it. But the boar swam across to Wales and fought off all attempts to take possession of it. Then it fled to the estuary of the River Severn, between Wales and England, and there the hunters had success. Mabon charged at the boar and snatched the razor from between his ears, and Cei managed to pluck away the scissors. Only the comb remained. The boar fled to Cornwall, where, after a mighty struggle, the comb was retrieved.

The knights returned to Ysbaddaden's castle. There they presented him with the razor, comb, and scissors, and the giant's beard was shaved off to the bone. Ysbaddaden then presented Olwen to Culhwch. The giant then met a grisly fate. Goreu, the herdsman's sole surviving son, grabbed him by the hair, cut off his head, and stuck it on a stake for all to see. Meanwhile, Culhwch rode off with the beautiful Olwen. They soon got married and lived happily together.

KING ARTHUR

The tale of Culhwch and Olwen contains one of the earliest mentions of the legendary King Arthur. In the later Middle Ages, many stories about Arthur were circulated. They told of his famous Knights of the Round Table, the love of Sir Lancelot for Arthur's wife, Guinevere, and the search for the Holy Grail—the chalice, or vessel, used at the Last Supper by Jesus Christ which was believed to have collected his blood while he was on the cross.

Scholars still debate whether a real, historical Arthur lay behind the figure of myth and legend. Some believe there was a warrior named Arthur who lived around the fifth century C.E., at a time when the Roman legions had left Britain and returned to Rome. This left the country defenseless against invaders, who included Angles and Saxons from northern Europe. Arthur may well have been a British or Welsh leader of the resistance against these invaders. Then in later times, he may have been dimly remembered as a famous warrior, and legends were woven around his name.

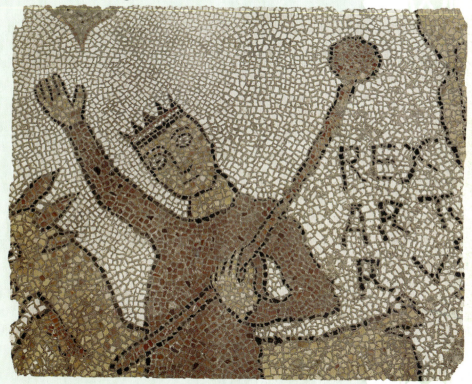

Above: The legend of King Arthur spread beyond England and Wales. He carries a scepter—the symbol of a king—and rides a goat in this medieval mosaic from Otranto Cathedral in Italy. Part of the Latin inscription, "Rex Arturus" (King Arthur), can be seen to the right.

TIMELINE OF THE CELTS

c. 900–450 B.C.E.

The early period of Celtic culture and art known as Hallstatt, named after an archaeological site in modern Austria, comes to the fore in central Europe.

c. 800–400 B.C.E.

The Celtic culture and language reach Britain and Ireland.

753 B.C.E.

Traditionally, the year the city of Rome is founded. Over the centuries, the city will develop into a superpower, conquering most of the Celtic world.

c. 600–500 B.C.E.

The grand Celtic hill-fort of Heuneburg, overlooking the Danube River in Germany, is thriving. The discovery of pottery and wine vessels has shown that the community was trading with the Greeks of Massilia (present-day Marseilles).

c. 550 B.C.E.

A Celtic chieftain is buried in a large mound at Hochdorf in Germany. The man was in his forties and stood just over 6 ft (1.8 m) tall. Objects surrounding him in the grave include arrows, fishhooks, gold brooches, a cauldron, drinking horns, and an ornate cup.

c. 500 B.C.E.

The Celts have established themselves in much of western Europe.

c. 450 B.C.E.

The La Tène style of Celtic art, characterized by curving, interlocking lines, begins to emerge. The style lasts until the first century B.C.E.

c. 390 B.C.E.

The Gauls (Celts living in what is now modern France) attack Rome. They demand a ransom of money to leave the Romans in peace. When the Romans complain about the amount of gold being weighed to give to the Gauls, the Gallic leader, Brennus, is said to have thrown his sword onto the scales with the shout, "Vae victis!" ("Woe to the conquered!").

c. 279 B.C.E.

A Celtic war band sacks the sacred site of Delphi in Greece.

c. 225–100 B.C.E.

Celts in France and Spain begin to suffer from attacks by Germanic tribes and Roman armies.

58–51 B.C.E.

The great Roman general Julius Caesar undertakes his conquest of Gaul. He conducts an efficient, clever campaign and annexes the whole region.

55–54 B.C.E.

Julius Caesar lands on British soil, but he does not stay long enough to conquer the island.

52 B.C.E.

The Gallic chieftain Vercingetorix revolts against Rome. After a victory against the Romans, he is besieged at the hilltop fortress of Alesia. There Caesar starves him into submission. He is taken to Rome and later executed.

43 C.E.

The Roman emperor Claudius orders an invasion of Britain. Within fifty years, the Romans have conquered most of Britain, but Ireland and much of Scotland escape invasion.

c. 60 C.E.

The British chieftain Boudicca (Boadicea) revolts against the Romans. She leads her Celtic warriors against the Roman settlements of Colchester, London, and St. Albans, burning buildings and slaughtering the inhabitants. She is eventually crushed by a force under Suetonius, the Roman governor of Britain. Boudicca poisons herself to avoid being taken alive.

350–600 C.E.

Significant numbers of Irish (who are known as Scotti) raid and settle in the west of Scotland.

c. 400–500 C.E.

The Roman Empire begins to collapse as Germanic tribes, including the Goths, Vandals, and Burgundians, take over large parts of the territory.

432 C.E.

St. Patrick begins his mission to convert the Irish to Christianity. He is not the first Christian to preach to the Irish, but his name will live on as the most effective missionary. Ireland will become a powerhouse of Christianity.

c. 450–600 C.E.

The Germanic peoples known as Angles, Saxons, and Jutes invade Britain, but Celtic peoples still survive in Wales, Cornwall, and parts of Scotland. During this time, numbers of Britons settle in the present-day region of Brittany, in northwest France.

c. 563 C.E.

St. Columba sails from his native Ireland and settles on the island of Iona off the west coast of Scotland. There he founds a monastery that will become famous for its spirituality. From his island base, he will travel to the Scottish mainland to convert the local people.

793 C.E.

The Vikings—fierce raiders from Scandinavia— sack the monastery of Lindisfarne, on the northeast coast of Britain. This date traditionally marks the beginning of the Viking Age, when Vikings attacked and settled in various parts of Europe over a period of 200 years.

794 C.E.

The Vikings attack Iona. It is the first of several raids that the island will suffer at Viking hands.

c. 800 C.E.

The *Book of Kells*, a masterpiece of Celtic-Christian art, is created. It was probably started on Iona and completed at the monastery of Kells in present-day County Meath in Ireland.

c. 1000–1100 C.E.

The story of St. Brendan's voyage is written down in Latin as the *Navigatio Brendani*. The tale will become a medieval bestseller.

c. 1300–1400 C.E.

Two Welsh manuscripts are created—*The Red Book of Hergest* and *The White Book of Rhydderch*— which bear the stories of the *Mabinogion*. The tales themselves are based on much older myths and legends.

GLOSSARY

ancient Greeks A people who lived mainly in what is now modern Greece. They became famed for their architecture, philosophy, literature, and other cultural achievements. Their civilization is often believed to have appeared around 1000 B.C.E. and lasted, in its classical form, until the end of the 300s B.C.E.

Angles An ancient Germanic people who invaded Britain during the fifth century C.E.

Annwn The Welsh Otherworld.

bard An ancient Celtic poet who wrote and recited poems.

Celts Any of a number of ancient peoples, including the Irish, Welsh, and Gauls, who originated in central Europe in the late Bronze Age (c. 1200–700 B.C.E.) and shared a similar language and culture. The spread of the Celtic languages to Ireland and Britain probably took place during the first half of the first millennium B.C.E.

Christianity A monotheistic religion that emerged in Palestine in the first century C.E., based on the life and teachings of Jesus of Nazareth. Christianity took root in Wales after its Roman occupiers officially adopted the religion in the fourth century C.E., and it reached Ireland in the following century.

cycle A group of traditional stories based around a theme or place.

druid A Celtic priest and law-giver.

Eisteddfod An annual festival held in Wales, which celebrates Welsh poetry and song.

Fianna The legendary elite warrior band who served the Irish king. The most famous leader of the Fianna was Finn Mac Cumhaill.

Gae Bolga Cuchulainn's spear, which he threw using his foot.

Gaul Roman name for the Celtic lands in France and northern Italy. The Roman conquest of Gaul was completed by Julius Caesar in 58–51 B.C.E.

geis An obligation that was placed on someone and meant he or she had to carry out or refrain from doing a particular action.

Hallstatt The early Celtic culture that existed from about the ninth to the fifth century B.C.E.

hurling An ancient Celtic field sport, still played in Ireland.

illumination A painted design or picture on the page of a manuscript.

La Tène The Celtic culture that existed from the fifth to the first century B.C.E.

Mabinogion A medieval collection of Welsh myths.

medieval Also referred to as the Middle Ages, the medieval period is commonly taken to begin c. 500 C.E. with the fall of the Western Roman Empire and to continue until c. 1500, the beginning of the early modern period.

mortar A mixture of natural materials used to bind together stones or bricks.

Ogham A form of writing, using straight lines, used by the ancient Celts.

Picts A group of tribes who were pre-eminent in Scotland in early Christian times until about the ninth century C.E.

Romans An ancient people, based in Italy, who carved out a great empire that eventually stretched from northern Britain to North Africa. The Roman Republic was established around 509 B.C.E. The Western Roman Empire, including Britain, Gaul, and Italy, broke down into independent kingdoms in the fifth century C.E. The last Western emperor was deposed in 476 C.E., the date historians usually give for the fall of the Roman Empire.

St. Patrick A Roman-Briton who is credited with converting the Irish to Christianity during the fifth century C.E.

Saxons An ancient Germanic people who, like the Angles, invaded Britain during the fifth century C.E.

sidhe "Fairy mounds" dotting the landscape of Ireland, beneath which are supposed to have lived the supernatural Tuatha De Danann.

Tara Stronghold of the High Kings of Ireland, in present-day County Meath.

torc A circular metal necklace, open at the front.

tribute Money or valuable goods given to indicate submission to a lord or to buy protection.

Tuatha De Danann A supernatural people who are said to have invaded Ireland and were eventually defeated by the Milesians.

votary offering An offering, such as money or a precious object, given to the gods.

warrior light A glowing light that shone above the head of Cuchulainn when his battle frenzy came upon him.

FOR MORE
INFORMATION

BOOKS
The following is a selection of books that have been used in the making of this volume, plus recommendations for further reading.

Bellingham, David. *An Introduction to Celtic Mythology*. London: Grange Books, 1990.

Berresford Ellis, Peter. *The Ancient World of the Celts*. London: Constable, 1998.

Chadwick, Nora. *The Celts*. Harmondsworth: Penguin Books, 1970.

Gantz, Jeffrey (trans.). *Early Irish Myths and Sagas*. Harmondsworth: Penguin Books, 1981.

Gantz, Jeffrey (trans.). *The Mabinogion*. Harmondsworth: Penguin Books, 1976.

Green, Miranda J. *Dictionary of Celtic Myth and Legend*. London: Thames & Hudson, 1992.

Heaney, Marie. *Over Nine Waves*. London: Faber & Faber, 1994.

James, Simon. *Exploring the World of the Celts*. London: Thames & Hudson, 1993.

Kinsella, Thomas. *The Tain*. Oxford: Oxford University Press, 1969.

MacCana, Proinsias. *Celtic Mythology*. London: Hamlyn, 1970.

Matthews, John and Caitlin Matthews. *The Encyclopaedia of Celtic Myth and Legend*. London: Rider, 2002.

Neeson, Eoin. *Celtic Myths and Legends*. Cork: Mercier Press, 1998.

O'Farrell, Padraic. *Ancient Irish Legends*. Dublin: Gill & Macmillan, 1995.

Powell, T.G.E. *The Celts*. London: Thames & Hudson, 1980.

Raftery, Barry. *Pagan Celtic Ireland*. London: Thames & Hudson, 1994.

Ritchie, W.F. and Ritchie, Graham. *Celtic Warriors*. Aylesbury: Shire Publications, 1985.

Rolleston, T.W. *Celtic Myths and Legends*. London: Studio Editions, 1994.

Zaczek, Iain. *Chronicles of the Celts*. London: Collins & Brown, 1996.

WEB SITES
www.timelessmyths.com
For Irish and Welsh myths. Contains short articles discussing Celtic history and aspects of the different stories.

www.sacred-texts.com/neu/celt/mab/index.htm
For the stories of the *Mabinogion*. It uses the English translation published by Lady Charlotte Guest in 1877.

www.bbc.co.uk/wales/celts
The site includes information about the Celts, a quiz, suggestions for making Celtic patterns, and other craft ideas.

www.maryjones.us/ctexts/index_irish.html
For Irish myths. The site is divided into a number of categories, including the Mythological, Ulster, and Fenian cycles, with individual stories listed. A variety of English translations is given.

www.sacred-texts.com/neu/cool
For the Cattle Raid of Cooley. The site divides the story into twenty-nine chapters. The English translation is from *The Ancient Irish Epic Tale Táin Bó Cúalnge* by Joseph Dunn.

MUSEUMS
The Keltenmuseum, Germany
www.keltenmuseum.de
This displays objects that were discovered in the grave mound of the Celtic chieftain buried at Hochdorf.

The British Museum, UK
www.thebritishmuseum.ac.uk
Here can be found the remains of Lindow Man, the ornate Celtic shield found in the Thames near Battersea, and other Celtic objects.

Trinity College Library, Ireland
www.tcd.ie/library
The college has a special exhibition displaying the *Book of Kells*.

The National Museum of Ireland, Ireland
www.museum.ie
A magnificent collection of pagan and Christian Celtic objects, including the gold ship from the Broighter Hoard and the Ardagh Chalice.

The National Museum Wales, Wales
www.museumwales.ac.uk/en/home/
A selection of Celtic objects, including fine examples of La Tène-style decoration.

INDEX

ACKNOWLEDGMENTS

Sources: AKG = akg-images, London **TIIC =** Irish Image Collection **Scala** = Scala, Florence **WF** = Werner Forman Archive

b = bottom c = center t = top l = left r = right

Front cover: top WF/British Museum, London; **bottom** The Irish Image Collection

Back cover: left WF/British Museum; **right** The Irish Image Collection

Pages: 1&2–3 TIIC **3c** AKG/Keltenmuseum, Austria; **7&10** IIC; **12** WF/National Museum of Ireland; **13** WF/British Museum; **15** Corbis/ Richard Cummins; **17** Scala/National Museum, Prague; **18-19** TIIC; **20c** WF/Musées de Rennes; **20b** Historisches Museum Bern; **21t&b** Scala; **23** IIC; **25** akg-images/Erich Lessing; **27** Scala/British Library; **28-29** WF/National Museum of Ireland; **30–33** TIIC; **34** Lord Price Collection; **37** Alamy/Peter Adams Photography; **38** Ancient Art & Architecture; **41t&b** Scala/British Museum; **42** IIC; **44–45** WF/British Museum, London; **46–47** Rex Features/Alisdair Macdonald; **49** Scala; **50–51** WF/British Museum; **52** Alamy/Ian M Butterfield; **53t** Manchester Museum; **53b** Scala/British Museum; **55** WF/British Museum; **56** TIIC; **57** Scala/British Library; **58** TIIC; **61** WF; **62** Lord Price Collection **65** TIIC; **67** Scala/Ann Ronan Picture Library; **68t** Scala/ Rheinisches Landesmuseum, Bonn; **68b** WF/Musée Archéologique de Breteuil; **69t** Bridgeman Art Library/National Museum of Ireland; **69b** Art Archive; **71** Collections/Michael Duggan; **72** Art Archive/Musée de la Civilisation Gallo-Romaine, Lyons/Dagli Orti; **74** Jean Williamson/Mick Sharp Photography; **77** Corbis/Farrell Grehan; **79** Bridgeman Art Library/ Musée Historique et Archeologique, Orleans; **81** Art Archive/Museo Nazionale Atestino Este/Dagli Orti; **82** Bridgeman Art Library/Musée de la Vieille Charite, Marseille; **83** © Alan Lee; **84–85** WF/National Museum, Copenhagen; **87** © Alan Lee; **89** Scala/Otranto Cathedral